Career
Q&A

Career Q&A

A Librarian's Real-Life, Practical Guide to Managing a Successful Career

Susanne Markgren and
Tiffany Eatman Allen

ⅲ Information Today, Inc.
Medford, New Jersey

First Printing, 2013

Career Q&A: A Librarian's Real-Life, Practical Guide to Managing a Successful Career

Copyright © 2013 by Susanne Markgren and Tiffany Eatman Allen

Publisher's Note: The authors and publisher have taken care in the preparation of this book but make no expressed or implied warranty of any kind and assume no responsibility for errors or omissions. No liability is assumed for incidental or consequential damages in connection with or arising out of the use of the information or programs contained herein.

Many of the designations used by manufacturers and sellers to distinguish their products are claimed as trademarks. Where those designations appear in this book and Information Today, Inc. was aware of a trademark claim, the designations have been printed with initial capital letters.

Library of Congress Cataloging-in-Publication Data

Markgren, Susanne, 1971-
  Career Q&A : a librarian's real-life, practical guide to managing a successful career / Susanne Markgren and Tiffany Eatman Allen.
      pages cm
  Includes bibliographical references and index.
  ISBN 978-1-57387-479-3
  1. Library science--Vocational guidance. 2. Librarians--Employment. 3. Career development. I. Allen, Tiffany Eatman, 1972- II. Title.
  Z682.35.V62M34 2013
  020.23--dc23

2013025623

Printed and bound in the United States of America

President and CEO: Thomas H. Hogan, Sr.
Editor-in-Chief and Publisher: John B. Bryans
Managing Editor: Amy M. Reeve
Project Editor: Rachel Singer Gordon
Editorial Assistant: Brandi Scardilli
VP Graphics and Production: M. Heide Dengler
Book Designer: Kara Mia Jalkowski
Cover Designer: Lisa Conroy

infotoday.com

Thanks to my parents, who have supported me through all my crazy endeavors (and long-distance moves). Thanks to my colleagues (past and present), who have listened to my (sometimes foolish and often grandiose) ideas and encouraged me to pursue alternative roles and to "put myself out there." Finally, thanks to Matt, Violette, Cecylia, and Boden for giving me the motivation and strength to try new things. You are constant reminders that flexibility, curiosity, and a sense of humor are keys to survival.

—Susanne

To my friends and family, thank you for your cheers, support, and confidence. (That's you, Mom and Dad!) Thanks also to my colleagues at work, especially my supervisor, who gave me time and encouragement (and a sympathetic ear when I started to panic). For all my CALAs—past, present, and future—your questions and curiosity are the reasons we've written this book. Go forth and be excellent! And lastly, thanks to Ricardito, one of the best friends a girl could hope for.

—Tiffany

CONTENTS

ACKNOWLEDGMENTS

It is with great appreciation that we recognize the following people for their help, support, and contributions to the book.

First and foremost, our thanks to Rachel Singer Gordon. Ten years ago, she selected the two of us to be co-authors of the advice column "Career Q&A With the Library Career People." Since then, she has provided guidance and encouragement, and she gave us the nudge we needed to write this book. Not only is she a friend and a mentor; she is an amazing editor.

Second, it is with sincere gratitude that we recognize our column readers. We have the pleasure of reading your questions each month and responding to them, knowing that there are many others out there with the exact same question or in a very similar situation. Thank you for seeking our advice and asking your questions—and be sure to keep them coming!

We would also like to thank everyone who responded to our survey for the book. It was lengthy and in-depth, and we thought that might dampen your enthusiasm for responding. However, we felt all the questions were important, and clearly you did, too. We received more than 2,300 responses, with an 81 percent completion rate. Thank you for sharing your thoughts, comments, advice, and experiences.

We are very grateful to our friends at Information Today. This book would not be possible without the guidance, (extreme) patience, and careful editing of John Bryans and Amy Reeve.

Last, we'd like to recognize our contributing authors, whose personal experiences, opinions, and guidance make the book more useful and interesting. We can't thank you enough.

ABOUT THE WEBSITE

librarycareerpeople.com

The Library Career People website highlights upcoming events and workshops that we are involved in; publications and presentations that are relevant to librarians and their careers; and data and responses (much more than we could fit into the book) from our career survey. Most importantly, the website contains 10 years' worth of Career Q&As—several of which are used throughout the book as jumping-off points for specific sections and chapters. This book would not have happened without the Career Q&As, which first appeared as a column in the *Info Career Trends Newsletter* in 2003.

We like to think of the website as a career development tool and archive of professional guidance and advice for librarians, library staff, and those thinking of entering the profession. If you have a question about the profession, please submit it on the website. Also email us at librarycareerpeople@gmail.com with any comments or questions, and follow us on Twitter (*@LibCareerPeople*).

Disclaimer

FOREWORD

When I consider the many aspects of my work—professional service, research, writing—I have no doubt that the most fulfilling experience is the small part I play in preparing the entry-level librarian for his or her first professional position. While one piece of this work as an educator is the planning and delivery of formal coursework, the occupation of educator is much more expansive and encompasses the roles of guide, advisor, and mentor. Hopefully, all of these actions are contributing factors to student graduation and subsequent employment. My happiest day, and undoubtedly my students' best day, is when I hear the good news that one of them has just accepted a job, doing what they want in the place where they want to be. When students graduate, our relationship is rebuilt. The power hierarchy shifts and levels so that we become peers. In many ways, I become the student as I come to rely on the alumnus to help me refresh my learning and share the new learning with the next entering student.

If I were to invent a perfect adjunct to the work I do, it would be a career management bible. It would be an advice column of sorts, offering the voice of the confident, kind, and helpful practitioner. It would be, in short, this book, *Career Q & A*, and how right it is that one of the co-authors is one of my former students. We could all use some help with the life of our careers.

A book like *Career Q&A* promotes reflection as well. My own path from a career as a medical imager/x-ray tech led to a course of studies designed to help me proceed into a career as a medical librarian. Then, turning down a position as a nursing specialist in an academic library to stay closer to my home at the time, I became an adult services librarian in a mid-sized public library. I left that position 2 years later to accept a last minute offer of a doctoral fellowship, leading to my position now as a professor at the University of Texas at Austin. Still, I have often contemplated the divergences in my career path, wondering what might have happened if I had entered into medical librarianship, accepted the nursing specialist position, or, at some point, sought an administrative position at a graduate program in another institution of higher learning. This contemplation is not one of regret but certainly has a small degree of wistful wondering of what might have been.

I have found that getting closer to retirement involves not only financial planning but also mental preparation. For me, this is a time of sorting out for a final time the pathway of choices, decisions, and alternatives to, hopefully, a stage of completion and satisfaction. How would I have used the advice from this book had it existed when I had started my career? Would the book have given me the encouragement at the right moment to go somewhere else with the career I found? All I know is that when I felt stuck, unappreciated, undervalued, and underpaid, I continued to find rewarding work with class after class of new students and the opportunities to explore new work areas and professional experiences. The refreshing of my work involved such activities as delivering new books to children attending tribal schools, joining a group of advisors in identifying global exemplars of love and forgiveness, helping select recipients of the awards and grants, involving libraries and librarians in film and music projects, and supporting the librarian community through serving as the 125th president of the American Library Association, the oldest and largest library association in the world. Whether your pathway in the ever changing and challenging field of librarianship will be similar to mine, this book will serve as a useful guide for the decisions you make now and throughout your career.

—Loriene Roy
School of Information, The University of Texas at Austin
Past President, ALA, 2007–2008

Introduction

Some people know they want to become librarians and head straight for librarianship after college. Others stumble into the profession, sometimes as a second, third, or fourth career choice. We all have different reasons for choosing librarianship, and we all experience different challenges as we transition through our careers.

The purpose of this book is to take a broad look at librarianship by dissecting it into different stages and answering specific questions about the various stages, events, transitions, struggles, and advances that encompass and define a librarian's career. Librarianship can be an exciting and rewarding career choice because it offers variety, flexibility, and growth. This book will share practical advice, experience, and information that can help librarians manage a successful and satisfying career.

Who Are We?

We are working librarians with more than 30 years' experience between us. We have worked in a variety of roles in different types of libraries all over the country. Like most people, we have families and responsibilities, deadlines and goals, troubles and worries. We have served on hiring committees, and we have interviewed for positions. We are members of library committees and associations. We are mentors. We have written, presented, and taught classes on myriad aspects of career management. Together, we have written the advice column "Career Q&A With the Library Career People" since 2003, answering a broad range of questions from librarians and information professionals, library school students, and people thinking about entering librarianship. You may already know us as the Library Career People. Because the idea for this book came out of our advice column and all of the questions and comments we have received over the years, we thought it would be fitting to begin each chapter with a library career question and to scatter some of the most frequently asked questions throughout the book.

The Stage

The stage is a metaphor for your career. Think of the stage as a platform where you will discover and create, engage, learn, and teach. Think of it as a setting in which to find your voice, hone your skills, shake off your fears, gain experience, acquire knowledge, and develop relationships. It carries you throughout your career and showcases many acts, characters, and intermissions (and some dramas and comedies) along the way.

We have divided the book into three parts. Part One, "Setting the Stage," focuses on getting started (or restarted) in the profession and on preparing yourself and your materials. It covers questions about finding jobs, composing cover letters, building resumes and portfolios, managing online identities, and interviewing.

Part Two, "Staging Your Own Set," is all about transitions and shaping your career into what you want it to be. We look at how librarians can move into different roles, how they can negotiate flexible hours and alternative schedules, and how they can form networks and gain confidence in their jobs.

Part Three, "Finishing Stages," is for working librarians who may be wondering, what next? It discusses staying current, moving up the career ladder, dealing with mid- and late-career dilemmas, forming collaborations, and preparing for retirement. The chapters, although arranged more or less according to the stages of a career, do not need to be read in order. Readers are encouraged to jump around and dip in as their needs and interests dictate.

And the Survey Says ...

Janet C., a librarian in a biomedical research library, commented:

> *If you want a successful career in librarianship— or just about anything else—you have to manage it. You can't just sit back passively and let things happen to you. You have to be proactive and figure out what you want; where you want to be in 2, 5, or 10 years; and what it will take to get there. Then start working on it.*

Profiles

We have had the good fortune, in our varied careers, to meet an array of successful, engaging, and inspiring librarians who have gone through transitions, made sacrifices, and challenged themselves to learn, create, succeed, and stay motivated. A number of them (19 to be exact) have contributed short essays, interviews, or profiles for this book. You will find their contributions in almost every chapter, in sidebars titled "Voice of Experience." A full list of contributors is included in Appendix A.

The Survey

In late 2011, we sent the survey "Career Q&A: Managing a Successful Career in Librarianship" (reproduced in Appendix C) to multiple email lists and social media sites (Facebook, Twitter, LinkedIn, and several blogs); it was then shared, promoted, and resent to other sites and lists. By early 2012, 2,369 people had started it, and 1,922 had completed it, for an 81 percent completion rate.

We developed the survey because we felt our readers would want to know what their colleagues and peers are saying about the issues we discuss, and we wanted to give survey respondents a chance to add their own advice and comments to our book. Throughout the chapters, their words appear in sidebars titled "And the Survey Says ..." Our survey respondents trend as follows:

- 84 percent are women.

- 95 percent are working in the U.S., 4 percent in Canada, and 1 percent in other countries.

- 27 percent are between the ages of 50 and 59, 25 percent between the ages of 30 and 39, 22 percent between the ages of 40 and 49, 13 percent between the ages of 60 and 69, 12 percent between the ages of 20 and 29, and 1 percent are 70 and older.

- 91 percent of the respondents have an MLS or equivalent.

- 77 percent are currently employed in a position that requires an MLS, and 33 percent have at least one graduate degree besides an MLS.

- 90 percent are working full-time.

- 41 percent are working in places with fewer than 10 staff members, 25 percent in places with 10 to 30 staff members, 19 percent in places with 31 to 100 staff members, and 15 percent in places with more than 100 staff members.

- 52 percent of respondents have interviewed for or started a new job in the past 2 years.

- 43 percent work in academic libraries, 23 percent in special libraries, 13 percent in public libraries, 4 percent in school libraries, and 9 percent in other libraries, while 8 percent are currently not employed in libraries.

Let's begin with Act 1, Scene 1: Setting the Stage.

Part One
Setting the Stage

"I had no idea of the character. But the moment I was dressed, the clothes and the make-up made me feel the person he was. I began to know him, and by the time I walked onto the stage he was fully born."

—Charlie Chaplin

THE BEGINNING: GETTING STARTED OR GETTING GOING

Dear Q&A: I'm on the market. For a job, that is. What do I need to know before I get started? And how can I find a job I love?

"Getting started" can mean different things to different people at different stages of their careers. It may mean getting restarted in a new role or new workplace, starting again after an absence from the profession, starting on the next step of one's career, or starting fresh after graduating from library school. No matter where you may be in your professional life, getting started is an exciting yet often frightening process that requires planning, motivation, and patience.

Setting Goals

Regardless of what's next for you in your professional life—around the corner, down the road, or in the distant future—it is always a good idea to have solid, written-out, well-defined goals. This is true even if those goals are always changing or end up getting pushed out the window by something else entirely. Having goals helps propel you from one place to the next, one role to the next, and one level to the next. Achieving your goals can help keep you motivated and satisfied in your career choices and give you momentum to do more. As Stephen Covey says about the habits of highly effective people, "Your life doesn't just *happen*. Whether you know it or not, it is carefully designed by you. The choices, after all, are yours ... Just remember that every moment, every situation, provides a new choice. And in doing so, it gives you a perfect opportunity to do things differently to produce more positive results."[1]

Even if you have no plans of leaving your wonderful job or no desire to move up in your career (or if there is no moving up to be had), you can still start something new. Identify something that you've been excited about learning, something that uses your unique set of skills and expertise, or something that will introduce you to new people and new opportunities. Librarians have many outlets, choices, and different ways to start anew.

How can you organize your goals? Start by making a simple list of what you want to achieve in your career. Be as specific or as broad as you like. Once you have a list, organize it into short- and long-term goals. Then create a list of things you need to do in order to achieve your goals. This list might include steps such as taking classes, getting an additional degree or certification, acquiring specific experiences, or overcoming anxieties or fears. Your list will probably be longer and more detailed for your long-range goals. For instance, if you aspire to be a library director, you will need to put in the time, gain supervisory and budgeting experience, attain another degree or certification, and so on.

This is a working list, so add to or edit it on a regular basis, and reward yourself when you make steps toward your goals. Share your list, or parts of your list, with colleagues. Get feedback, ideas, and support from those you know. By sharing your goals with others, you are making those goals real, giving them power, and putting more pressure on yourself to actually achieve them. (See Chapter 11 for more information on career planning and goal setting.)

Sample Career Goals Template

Career Goals (in priority order)	Measurements	Steps to Take	Time Frame
Goal 1: Create an online portfolio or a professional web presence.	Gather feedback from colleagues and data from website analytics and statistical tools.	- Find out about potential (and free) tools to use. - Learn basic HTML skills (take a class if needed). - Gather/digitize/organize materials to put online. - Start building my portfolio.	1 month
Goal 2: Start a mentoring program for new librarians at my library.	Gather ongoing feedback from participants and formal assessment at the end of the program.	- Write down mission and goals, and plan for the program. - Get feedback, buy-in, and support from director and colleagues and potential mentors. - Develop an assessment tool.	3 months
Goal 3: Complete a second master's degree in order to move into a higher position.	Enroll in a degree program, and complete one class per semester and one each summer.	- Get support from my family. - Get support from my employer (flextime and/or financial support). - Acquire/identify funds to pay for classes and materials.	4–5 years

Whether we are fresh out of library school or long-term veterans of the profession, the No. 1 goal for many of us is finding a job. And not just any job, but a job that we like; that we enjoy doing; that we can grow in, learn from, and feel proud of; and that will enhance our skill sets and propel our careers. But the process of finding a job can be a long and difficult journey. Before beginning any job search, start by doing some prep work. Ask yourself questions such as, Am I geographically mobile? Where would I like to live? What type of jobs will I apply for? What types of libraries do I want to work in? What types of people do I want to work with? Am I flexible with my hours? How much money do I need to survive in XYZ city? How important is professional development? Where do I want to be in 5 or 10 years? What is my time frame for securing a job? Would I take a nonlibrarian position? Would I take a part-time or temporary position? Would I consider a job outside of libraries? How do I define myself professionally?

The answers to these questions will assist you in visualizing and formalizing your professional goals, which will make your job search easier and help guide you in your path toward a successful career.

Searching for a Job

Among the many career-related questions we receive from librarians, the most common ones are, How do I find a job? and Why *can't* I find a job? To these questions, we have many answers, and we'll outline some of them in this chapter. Each person has a unique set of experiences and skills, and each job is different. Ideally, you will want to find the right job at the right time for you. When you apply and interview for a position, you will want to sell yourself as the right person for *that particular job*. Also, keep in mind that most people don't find their dream job right away. The path to your dream job will most likely involve several jobs, roles, levels, and locations.

Geographic Mobility or Lack Thereof

Being able to move for a job, or being geographically mobile, will open up your job search. This makes it much easier to find jobs that interest you and are the right fit. If you are able to move for a job, here are a few tips:

- *Be choosy.* Find a place or area that you actually like, or a city where you want to live. Your original plan might be to move and work someplace for a year or two and then move back or move somewhere else. However, even if you have no intention of staying permanently, keep in mind that something may end up keeping you there longer than you had planned. Do your homework on the area, and you'll have a better chance of getting the job. Employers want to know that a candidate really wants to live in their area. You need to sell yourself and your skills for the job, but you also need to sell your interest in the location.

- *Use your connections.* Do you have friends, relatives, colleagues, or online connections who live in, or are familiar with, an area you might want to move to? You never know what kind of support, tips, advice, referrals, introductions, and recommendations you may get from these contacts. They can influence your job search and perhaps offer incentives for moving to the area.

- *Don't spend a ton of (your own) money.* When offered interviews in different cities, states, provinces, or countries, ask about reimbursement of travel expenses or about alternatives to travel, such as conducting the interview via an online video tool. For final interviews, however, most employers will want to meet you in person; likewise, you will want to meet them in person and physically explore the library, its collections, and the geographical area to make sure you will fit into a specific environment before you make the decision to move. When it comes to interviewing in person, some institutions will cover travel expenses to bring you in for an interview, but others will not. If you are considering interviewing with an institution that does not pay for travel and lodging, figure out how much the travel will cost you and think about how much you want the job and want to move to that specific area. Then weigh your options, keeping in mind that you will most likely go on many interviews before you get a job offer.

If you are *not* geographically mobile, remember that as you chart your course, every step builds on the next. When you take a job in a new place, you are starting fresh on a new adventure. When you stay put, your path has already begun. You need to arm yourself with the familiar: experiences, skills, and people you know. As you move along your career path in a given location, always assume that employers know one another; you might be surprised at how small the library world is, even in the biggest of cities. You will also need more patience because there will be fewer job openings when you are geographically constrained. Here are some tips for nonmobile job seekers:

- *Take advantage of your existing professional relationships.* This can include library school professors, colleagues, or supervisors from student jobs or past jobs, and people you interact with on committees, working groups, or other types of networks. Stay connected with these people and let them know you are looking for a job. They can serve as references and may be able to review your professional materials, refer you for a job, and offer valuable advice about local libraries and employers.

- *Seek out local internships or volunteer opportunities at a library in your area*, preferably one where you could see yourself working. Since it might take time to find a job, you can get experience and make connections at the same time.

- *Join local associations and groups as soon as you can.* Get involved in professional development opportunities in your area. Not only will you connect with others in your community who may be able to help you find a job or serve as references, but you are building skills and keeping yourself motivated and active as a professional.

THOUGHTS ON STARTING A NEW JOB

Richard A. Murray, metadata librarian at Duke University Libraries and assistant editor of LIScareer.com

Accepting a job offer may be the most exciting part of a job search, but it's not the end; it's just the beginning. I've worked at three Association of Research Libraries (ARL) libraries during my 16 years in the profession, and I've learned that what you do during your first 6 months in a position is just as important as what you did while you were trying to get the job.

My first library job was a paraprofessional position that I stumbled into accidentally. Libraries had never occurred to me as a place I could actually work, and I saw the job as a way to pay the bills until I figured out what I actually wanted to do. I knew nothing when I started that job. By the time I started my second position, I'd earned an MLS while working full-time and knew a lot more, but probably not as much as I thought I did. And by the time I started my current job a few years later, I'd figured out that nobody knew everything, that sometimes I actually did know more about certain things than anybody else did, and that, to a large extent, we all make it up as we go along. That last part was simultaneously a liberating and terrifying realization. Along the way, I learned something new while starting each new job—some things the easy way and some the hard way—and here are a few things I wish somebody had told me early on.

It can be tempting, especially in your first professional position, to charge in with guns blazing and try to implement all the big ideas you have right away. You may see things during your first few months—or maybe even during your interview—that you want to change immediately. Resist that urge. Unless you're working in a single-person operation, you will have co-workers, many of whom have probably been in the profession longer than you have, and it's likely they won't appreciate it if you come charging in like a bull in a china shop and start turning everything upside down (even if they agree that those changes need to happen). Start building relationships, find out what your new colleagues feel is working and not working, and try to get others on board with changes before you start making them. Remember, you don't know everything, and you probably don't know as much as you think you do. That's OK. Try to minimize how much of your not-knowing-stuff you inflict on your new colleagues.

As you're establishing yourself in your new job, listen more than you talk. Look around to see who is well liked and who makes things happen in the organization, and try to figure out what they're doing that others respond well to. Introduce yourself to the power players and try to form relationships with them.

Every office, no matter how peaceful or amiable, has politics. The larger the organization, the more complicated the web of relationships will be. There are probably people who don't like each other. They may have invested many years in not liking each other, and they may try to get you to take sides in their feud. Don't get drawn into the morass. They've been fighting with each other for a long time without you, and they can continue without you. Remember that it is possible to be friends with two people who don't like each other.

It's likely there will be a rumor mill at your new job. Unless it's really toxic and out of control, this is not necessarily a bad thing. You can learn a lot about the organization by listening to what your colleagues are saying about it. Take it all with a grain of salt, but keep your ears open. You can stay plugged into the grapevine without contributing to it. You don't want to earn a reputation as someone who spreads gossip, but that doesn't mean you can't listen to it.

That's the negative side of interpersonal relationships in the office. There's a positive side, too. Librarianship is a diverse profession full of interesting, intelligent, genuinely nice people. I hope you'll be working with some of them in your new job. Take the time to get to know your new colleagues, including those outside your department with whom you may not work directly (yet). Eat lunch with them in the staff lounge from time to time. It will help you observe the way they interact, find out what is important to them, and also make some friends. It will also make them feel as if you're interested in them and are making an effort to become part of the team. This is especially important if you've relocated for the job and don't know many people in the community. Your new colleagues will probably be happy to answer your questions about the area. Discussing topics such as local restaurants, places to walk your dog, or fun day trips is an easy way to start making friends.

The first few months in any new job are stressful, but they should also be exciting, unpredictable, and fun. This is, after all, what you worked so hard to achieve. Take time to enjoy it, gain new experiences, and build positive relationships with your new colleagues, patrons, and community. And don't worry, you won't be the new kid forever—somebody newer will probably get hired for some other position before long, and then you'll get to be the veteran who shows them the ropes.

Getting a Job With Little or No Library Experience

The best way to get a job is to have (or have had) a job. This is the classic dilemma: You can't get a job without experience, and you can't get experience without a job. Most job ads say "experience required" or "experience preferred." It's no secret: Employers prefer candidates with prior experience working in a library, even for entry-level jobs. Ideally, you would try to get this experience before or during library school. This is where we jump up and down and yell "Experience, experience, experience!"

Working in a library before or during library school can be beneficial in many ways, not just in terms of acquiring experience to put on your resume, but also in figuring out what type of library you would like to work in or what type of career path you would like to pursue. (Or the reverse: learning what type of library or role you definitely do not want to pursue!) Having this knowledge ahead of time will help you focus your education and your job search and will help you tailor your experience and skills to the specific job you want.

Lack of experience, or lack of the right experience, is often one of the main reasons you may not be getting a job. If you've never worked in a library before, you can volunteer, intern, or look for a part-time or paraprofessional position. Here are some suggestions:

- *Find a local library and ask about volunteering.* Be prepared with an up-to-date resume and know what hours you can work. Volunteers usually cannot be picky about what tasks they do, but if you let the people in charge know that you are interested in learning about specific things, they may allow you to do more after they see the quality of your work.

- *Intern.* If you're still in school or are a recent grad, talk to your library school about opportunities. Even if you have graduated, you still might be able to do an "unofficial" internship. These positions may be paid or unpaid and are usually more clearly defined than volunteer positions; you'll work on a specific job or task for a limited amount of time. Alternatively, contact a local library on your own and ask about possible internships. Again, be prepared. Let them know about your area of interest and your skills, and offer to be of assistance on any special or ongoing projects.

- *Apply for a part-time or paraprofessional job.* If you don't have *any* library experience but you need to pay the bills, and you find a good (paying) job that helps you acquire the experience you need to find an MLS position later on, go for it. However, we typically don't recommend that people with library degrees apply for positions that don't require the MLS; taking a nondegreed position is potentially harmful to your career trajectory, as it sometimes raises red flags for potential employers and makes it more difficult to find a professional position later on.

Starting Again After an Absence

Everyone's situation is different, and many factors influence the decision to seek a new job or stay put. Ideally, we should all be happy in our workplace, keep learning new things, work in a supportive environment, find mentors, and get a paycheck. We wish this for all of you, but we also understand that at times, life throws curve balls. Situations can change, and you may find yourself out of work or working outside of a library for a time.

Starting over can be a challenge for anyone, and especially for those who have been out of the workforce for many years. Not only do you need to update your materials, you also need to update yourself. Your library degree and past experience do not expire, but skills can become outdated quickly in today's libraries. Employers want to hire candidates who are current and who are aware of recent trends, issues, and projects.

When you apply for positions, you will need to address your absence from the profession. Be prepared to do so, both in your cover letters and during interviews. Be honest and open in a professional manner, without sharing too much personal information. One person who wrote to "Career Q&A With the Library Career People" asked for help getting back into the workforce after an absence. She was "very aware that I cannot mention cancer ... or motherhood" in my cover letter. We responded sympathetically, and said that, in fact, she should mention both. Illness and parenthood are two of the most common reasons people leave the workforce. Overcoming an illness and becoming a parent are two huge accomplishments—and should be seen as such.

Gaps in your resume will stand out. If these gaps are not addressed, they will hurt your chances of getting a job. Unexplained gaps leave a potential employer wondering what you were doing during those times. So, explain yourself first, before they start to wonder. Be eloquent, be convincing, and make whoever reads your cover letter believe that you are ready to re-enter the workforce. Here are some things to consider while getting your materials, and yourself, up-to-date:

- *Stay connected.* You don't want to come off as waking up from a deep sleep. Stay aware of what's going on in the professional world, and show that you can and want to stay current with the news and literature. Follow influential people on Twitter, join professional discussion groups on LinkedIn, and develop a professional online identity.

- *Volunteer.* If possible, try to get some current library experience to make yourself more hirable. The easiest way to do this is to volunteer. Ask local libraries or related institutions whether they need assistance with specific projects.

- *Take classes.* Many online and on-campus courses are offered by library schools, associations, universities, and technology companies. Think about taking a few to get up-to-date with new technologies or to learn about new concepts or trends in the profession.

- *Consider and use transferable skills.* Don't discount the experience you've acquired during your absence from the workforce or experience from other jobs and roles that can translate into librarianship.

- *Have impeccable application materials (resume and cover letter).* Make sure your materials are professional and polished. You need to shine and stand out in every way possible.

- *Be confident and positive.*

The 7 Habits of Highly Effective People:[2]

Habit 1: Be Proactive
Habit 2: Begin With the End in Mind
Habit 3: Put First Things First
Habit 4: Think Win-Win
Habit 5: Seek First to Understand, Then to be Understood
Habit 6: Synergize
Habit 7: Sharpen the Saw

You're Hired! Now What?

So, you got the job. What happens now?

The First Day

Most of your first day will be spent getting to know people at work, getting paperwork done, and getting ready for work—not actually working. Remember that it's OK, and even expected, for you to ask questions. You'll also be meeting many new people on your first day and learning a lot of new names. In between meetings, if you can jot down names, responsibilities, and a brief note about the person (e.g., *John Smith, acquisitions, wears nice ties, is super friendly*), you'll have a much better chance of remembering details down the road.

The First Week

The first week is a time for you to get to know your work environment, the larger (parent) institution, and your colleagues a little better. Use this week to get to know the people you are going to be working with and to create relationships with people who will help you as you advance in your new role. Try to meet with people on an individual basis and ask them questions about their jobs, their goals, and their expectations of working with you. You will learn a lot about the workflow in the library, and you will make friends in the process. Also, use your new colleagues as sources of local information for neighborhood eateries, shops, and events. Set up lunch dates to get to know them better.

While you're meeting new people in your library, find out who else, outside your library and even outside your institution, might be good for you to meet. They may include people in the information technology department or librarians or library staff members in related libraries or consortia. Find out from your supervisor and your colleagues whom you should contact and start a list of names. While the first week is your chance to ask lots of questions and get to know the people you will be working with and for, it is also a time to impress others with your enthusiasm and eagerness to be a part of the team. Making a good first impression will benefit you in the future.

The First Month

The first month is when you really get to know the ins and outs of your role in the library and what is required of you. As you dive into your job responsibilities and get into the rhythm of the work environment, remember that you are still new and still in a trial or probationary period. Don't be afraid to ask for feedback from your supervisor and assistance from your colleagues, if needed. If you filled an existing position, collect and go through materials left behind by the previous person (e.g., files, papers, projects, notes). If you are in a newly created position, you'll need to work closely with your supervisor to develop goals that will fulfill the needs of the library and integrate this new position seamlessly into the team. Organize all your materials and your office space. Save everything at this point, because you don't know what you might need in the future.

The first month is also a good time for you to become involved in committees, associations, and groups, both those that interest you and ones that will assist you in your job. Ask about worthwhile groups or committees to join. You should also join online communities and subscribe to library-related blogs and email lists—places to learn new things and keep up-to-date on new resources and new technology.

You will certainly feel energized as you start your new job, and you might even feel like charging forward and getting things done quickly. Before you do, make sure you're not stepping on any toes, that you're not changing the workflow, and that you're not excluding others in the process. Many new librarians are hired as "change agents," with the expectation that they will motivate other staff members and bring in new ideas. Such change can be a very positive thing for a stale work environment, but it needs to be done gradually, and it requires clear goals, communication, support from management, and buy-in from the staff. Whether you are stepping into someone else's shoes or starting out in a newly created position, learn what is expected of you—and set your own job-specific and career-related goals for your first month, first year, and beyond.

Sticking to Your Goals

It's easy to tell people to set goals and work hard toward achieving them, but doing so isn't a simple process. Achieving your goals involves planning, reflection, and introspection—as well as setbacks and frustration. When you plan your career path and think about what you want to achieve and where you want to end up, you need to consider other life goals as well, such as your family, location, personality, and abilities. It's kind of like writing a book: You need to figure out what you want to include, attempt to organize and make sense of the various parts, gather external data and information, and start writing. And don't forget to give yourself a deadline. Panic may set it: Who are you to plan out your life and have such lofty aspirations, to think you can achieve your dreams? Our advice is to own it, live it, learn from your failures or setbacks, and keep going.

So what are you waiting for? Go. Get started already.

Endnotes

1. Stephen Covey, "The 7 Habits of Highly Effective People," accessed July 10, 2013, www.stephencovey.com/7habits/7habits.php.
2. Ibid.

2

MAKING A GOOD FIRST IMPRESSION: THE ART OF THE COVER LETTER

Dear Q&A: I've found a job I'm really interested in, and I'm getting ready to apply. How important is the cover letter? Any tips you can provide on how to write a good letter?

When you are applying for a job, the cover letter serves multiple purposes:

- An introduction
- A statement of interest
- A writing sample
- A marketing tool
- Most important, a first impression

Some people say that we've lost the art of letter writing. In our age of digital communication, very few people put pen to paper—so to speak—anymore. Messages and characters have trumped sentences and structure, and immediacy has overtaken quality. Our modes of communication will continue to change as technologies advance and users adapt, but we need to be careful not to lose touch with certain modes, such as the letter. Cover letters are required for job seekers and are still the preferred mode for conveying our work history, our skills, and our achievements to others.

The cover letter is an essential piece of any job application. It is not a superfluous document but deserves attention and care as a promotional tool that conveys the reasoning, justification, and personality behind your application materials. The cover letter introduces you and your resume to the hiring committee, and if done well, your cover letter can get your foot in the door for that coveted interview.

Let's admit it. Most of us have at some point in our job-seeking past written generic, lackluster cover letters. We'd then use that same letter for every job we might be somewhat qualified for, just changing the name and address at the top. We'd stick these letters in the mail along with an equally generic resume and cross our fingers. This never worked well, did it? Since those days, we have learned a lot about what not to do. Because we still see so many bad cover letters from job applicants and have received so many questions about cover letters, we'll share some tips to help you write letters that actually improve your chances.

The truth is that your cover letter can be, and often is, more important than your resume. Why? It's simple: Cover letters are read first. They are meant to be read before everything else in your application packet and to provide an introduction to you as a job candidate and to your application materials. Your cover letter ideally gives the reader an idea of who you are and why you are applying for a particular job.

Unfortunately, the wrong cover letter can make a very poor first impression on the hiring committee or a potential employer. Is your cover letter a desperate discourse on how much you need a job? Is it a generic letter with no substance? Does it contain errors? Did you copy and paste the wrong job title into it? Does it focus only on how great you are? These are all fantastic ways to disqualify yourself right off the bat. Your chances of getting that interview are slim, and you've essentially made your resume worthless. What a waste!

If only you had taken the time to write a thoughtful, interesting, and engaging cover letter. If only you had studied the job requirements and looked up information on the library and the institution. If only you had proofread the letter and made sure there were no spelling or grammatical errors. If only you had shown some interest in the actual job you were applying for. If only you had shown the reader why you are the right person for the job, rather than simply saying you are.

A cover letter needs to do three things:

1. Provide a statement of interest that convinces the reader (e.g., the hiring committee, director of human resources, library director) that you really want the job

2. Present a summary of your qualifications that relate directly to the job requirements

3. Serve as an effective writing sample

Statement of Interest or Intent

In the hundreds of cover letters we've read during the years, the No. 1 thing that job candidates fail to do is convince us that they really want the job. It seems so basic, right? Of course you want the job—you're applying for it! Why else go to the trouble of sending in your application materials? This may be true, but try to think, or read, from the perspective of someone who doesn't know you: the hiring committee. They read through dozens, sometimes hundreds, of resumes, looking for a good match to a specific job or role. When a candidate does not show interest in a specific job and relate his or her experience and skills to that specific job, the committee most likely will come to the conclusion that this candidate just needs a job, any job, not necessarily the job at hand.

A cover letter needs to convey interest from the very beginning, in the very first paragraph. You can do this by stating that you are interested in the job, which can be as simple as "I am very interested in the ABC librarian position at XYZ Library." This is only the beginning, however. You need to convey interest in the job throughout the cover letter, and you need to explain *why* you are interested.

One of the best ways to show interest in a particular job is to research the library, the librarians who work there, the institution, the library system, and the resources and services the library offers. Then use what you've learned to connect your skills and experience to *this particular library's environment and needs*. Let the hiring committee know that you've done your research and that you are interested in the position because of what you've learned. For example, let's say that you discover that XYZ Library recently started promoting its services and resources using various social media tools. You could say, "I noticed that you have started using this tool to promote your services. This is a wonderful way to communicate with users, and I am quite familiar and comfortable with using this tool. In my current job, I have used it to promote our classes and new items in our collection, and we've received positive feedback from our patrons." Remember, a little flattery goes a long way.

Summary of Your Qualifications

Your cover letter needs to summarize your experience and skills *as they relate to the job at hand*. It should take the relevant information from your resume and use that information to show that you are qualified for the position. So, when writing your cover letter, have a copy of the job requirements on hand. Look closely at the words that are used in the job ad, and use some of those same words in your cover letter. If the job ad asks specifically for experience using discovery tools, then you had better include the words "discovery tools" in your cover letter and be specific about which one(s) you have used. In a job ad, job requirements are typically ordered by importance, with the most important being first. You should follow this same format and address the most important job requirement first. If the requirement states that the candidate must have at least 5 years of academic library experience, then talk about your years of experience in one paragraph, using successive paragraphs to address other requirements.

A Writing Sample

As you write your letter, think back to your high school English classes. Vary your sentence structure and choice of words (e.g., do not start every sentence with "I"). Use proper punctuation. Do not misspell words. Be consistent and accurate in your use of verb tense (for a current position or job, use the present tense; for past jobs, use the past tense). Use active voice, rather than passive, whenever possible. Use your language to show, rather than tell.

When outlining your qualifications, avoid generalizations. Be specific! We can't tell you how many candidates use general and generic language in response to the job ad. Generalizations will kill your cover letter, as well as your chances of getting an interview. Even though generalizations are often used in job ads, do not use them in your cover letter. If the ad calls for someone with good communication skills, do not simply say "I have excellent communication skills." That tells the hiring committee nothing. Instead, say "I have been a member of several committees over the years. Through the use of internal wikis and staff training, we have developed a productive way to communicate with all committee members and others in the library."

And the Survey Says ...

Following is a just a sample of the answers we received to the question, What one piece of advice would you give someone about writing a cover letter?

- *Introduce yourself.*
- *Tailor the letter to the position you are applying for.*
- *Address the requirements and the environment of the job.*
- *State why you want the job.*
- *Do not repeat what is in your resume.*
- *Match your experience to the requirements.*
- *Avoid puffery, buzzwords, jargon, and superlatives.*
- *Demonstrate insight and courtesy by showing that you've researched the needs of the organization.*
- *Let your personality and your passion for the profession shine through.*
- *Tell stories that paint a picture.*
- *Remember that* how well you write is *(almost) as important as* what you write.
- *Spell correctly, use good grammar, and proofread (and proofread again).*
- *Have someone else review your cover letter before you send it out.*

Structure of a Cover Letter

Every cover letter should be different, but you should try to come up with a basic structure that you can follow in all your letters. Here is a sample template for any cover letter:

- *Paragraph 1:* State where you saw the job ad and include an initial sentence or two that states your interest in the position and explains why you are interested.

- *Paragraph 2:* Provide a summary of your current situation (e.g., your role and your library, organization, or institution).

- *Paragraph 3:* Address the first (and most important) job requirement and talk about specific examples to connect your experience and skills with the job you want.

- *Paragraph 4:* Address the next job requirement (or next few job requirements) and, again, talk about specific examples to connect your background with the job.

- *Paragraph 5:* Discuss other skills you have that are relevant to the job (these might be the "preferred" qualifications), and be specific. If the job requires technical skills, interpersonal skills, or foreign language skills, provide examples here.

- *Paragraph 6 (final paragraph):* Restate your interest in the job and thank the committee for its time and its consideration of your application. That's it. Do not say that you will call them. Do not say that you are best candidate for the job. Do not say that you look forward to interviewing with them. Just say thank you.

Common Cover Letter Mistakes

Here are a few common mistakes we've seen in cover letters over the years:

- *Displaying overconfidence:* There is a fine line between bragging and exuding confidence in your own abilities. Don't ever assume (or say) that you are the best candidate, because you're probably not. Your tone should be humble and appreciative, not cocky and assertive.

- *Misspelling words:* Misspelling is probably the most common mistake—and may be forgivable, to a degree. However, employers know that this is also the easiest mistake to fix. Make sure to proofread, spell check, and have someone else read your cover letter. Also, read it aloud. It can be easy to miss something when reading silently to yourself.

- *Addressing it to the wrong person:* This mistake shows that you didn't do your homework or didn't pay attention to the job ad. If the job ad doesn't provide a name, address your letter to the head of a department (*Dear Director of Human Resources*) or to the search committee (*Dear Search Committee Members*).

- *Using the wrong job title:* If you put the wrong job title in your cover letter, then you've blown it. This is a dead giveaway that your cover letter is mass-produced and generic. Search committees will most likely stop reading and move on to the next applicant.

- *Being dishonest:* If you claim to have done something that you didn't actually do, you will most likely be found out. People talk to each other, and lies will eventually be exposed. The search committee chair will have your cover letter in hand when he or she speaks to your references and will ask about specific things you did, or claimed to do, so be honest.

Common Questions About Cover Letters

In our column, we've answered many questions about cover letters. Here are some of the most common.

Q: Can a cover letter be more than one page? I've been told that it should always fit on one page.

This is a tricky question. Many people feel strongly that cover letters should be limited to one page, and for the most part we agree. But we also think that they can run onto a second page when well written and presenting relevant information. Sometimes you just need that extra paragraph or page to adequately relate your experience and skills to the job requirements, especially if you have a lot of experience or the job has many requirements. As a general rule, the more experience you have, the longer the cover letter will be. If you are a newer librarian and do not have much library experience, your letter should fit on one page.

Q: When emailing materials, should I put the cover letter in the body of the email or attach it?

Unless specifically told to include your cover letter in the body of the email, attach it as a separate document. Cover letters are printed out, copied, and passed along to several people. And cover letters have a certain appearance that you want to maintain; a cover letter pasted into the body of an email won't look like a letter. Simply include a brief note in the body of the email stating that you are attaching your cover letter and resume and thanking the recipients for their time and consideration.

Q: If I send my materials as an attachment, can I combine my cover letter and resume into one file?

No, always keep these documents separate. They exist on their own and have their own look, design, and integrity. Also, the hiring committee may think something is missing if they have only one document.

Q: Should I repeat what is in my resume?

No, your cover letter should expand on your resume, especially in terms of the skills and experience that relate to the job requirements. Your resume stands on its own, as a record of your employment, skills, achievements, education, and commitment to your profession and to the job you want. Your cover letter is a unique document written to a specific person, committee, library, or institution. It interprets your resume and introduces you as a job candidate.

Q: Should I ever use bullets in my cover letter?

This is a stylistic choice that really doesn't work for everyone, or every letter. Bullet points are typically used to draw attention to a list of items, which, in the case of a cover letter, may be skills, achievements, projects, or experience. It may be tempting to use them, but as a general rule, we don't recommend it. Remember that a cover letter is a writing sample, and if you are tempted to reduce sentences to one-word bullet points, think again. A potential employer wants to see that you know how to write and communicate, and you don't need to use visual cues or stylistic gimmicks. Save your bullet points, if you really want to use them, for your resume.

Q: How far in advance of getting my degree can I apply for a position? And how do I address this in my cover letter?

You can apply for positions before earning your degree if you will have met all the requirements by the time the job begins. For example, if a job ad states that the position starts in September and you will receive your degree in August, then go ahead and apply. Include an anticipated graduation date in the first or second paragraph of your cover letter. If the job ad does not provide a start date (and most will not), then go ahead and apply if you will be receiving your degree within 3 months. If the job starts before then, you may not get to the interview stage (because you won't yet meet all the requirements). However, most job searches take several months, so it doesn't hurt to apply now.

Q: Should my cover letter address gaps in my work history?

Yes, your cover letter is exactly the place. Gaps in your resume will stand out, and if they go unexplained, they will send up red flags. Don't leave the potential employer wondering; be direct and up-front. One or two lines will suffice; apologies aren't necessary. You could say something such as "After taking some time off to [fill in the blank], I am enthusiastic about returning to librarianship, and I'm especially excited about this opportunity at XYZ Library." The statement should be brief and slightly personal and convey optimism and confidence. Address the gap without going into detail.

Keys to a Good Cover Letter

In summary, here are the key take-aways to remember when writing a cover letter:

- Explain why you are right for the job.
- Mention where you saw the job ad.
- Relate your experience and skills to the job requirements.
- Explain gaps (if any) in your work history.
- Explain why you intend to (or want to) move for the job.
- Expand on one or two specific jobs, projects, or accomplishments that are relevant to the position.
- Highlight one or two related systems or tools that you have used in a current or previous job.
- Demonstrate that you can write well.
- Show potential employers that you know something about their library.
- Convince the reader that you really want the job.
- Be gracious.

3

DOCUMENTING YOUR EMPLOYMENT HISTORY: THE ART OF THE RESUME

Dear Q&A: I am applying for my dream job and have been asked to submit a cover letter and resume. I haven't done a resume in a while and feel like I could use a crash course in what to include and how to include it.

While the cover letter serves to introduce you and express your interest in a position, your resume provides the details that prove you are the right person for the job. The resume documents your employment history, your experiences and qualifications, and your career over time. Whether you are just getting started or have years of experience in the profession, the purpose of your resume remains the same: to document your educational credentials, on-the-job experience, and professional service and activity. While your cover letter will change from job to job and should be tailored for each position, your resume will remain fairly consistent over time. Your

31

resume will grow in length as your experience grows, but it is generally limited to four or five pages.

As a working document, your resume should reflect you and your experience. Resumes come in all shapes and sizes and in varying formats. The two most common types of resumes are chronological and functional. You will likely be more familiar with chronological resumes, which list your most recent experience first and work back in time.

In contrast, functional resumes are laid out by grouping similar experiences together. Functional resumes focus on experiences as a whole, rather than on when or where. For potential employers, one major drawback of the functional arrangement is difficulty gauging a candidate's depth of knowledge or experience. The employer is often unable to measure how *much* experience the candidate has and in what context.

As an example, let's say you've held three positions in the course of your career. In a chronological resume, you would present each position (including your title, dates of employment, name of the institution, and primary responsibilities of the position) in sequential order, beginning with the most recent. In a functional resume, you would instead group the responsibilities of each position together under common categories such as management, technology, or public services, describing in detail your work in each of those areas. Functional resumes can be useful for candidates who are switching careers or have employment history gaps and want to highlight specific skills and experience that are relevant to the job. Most employers, however, prefer the chronological format because it's easy to see an applicant's employment history take shape over time. The chronological resume also shows when skills and experiences were gained and applied, in what context, and for how long.

Resume vs. Curriculum Vitae

There is a lot of overlap between a resume and a curriculum vitae (CV). Both provide basic employment information, education credentials, and contact information. In the U.S., applicants are generally asked to submit a resume when applying for a position; the CV is more commonly used internationally and is also more common in academia. The CV may also include information not commonly included in the resume, such as date of birth, nationality, and summaries of experience and research specialization. With this additional information, the CV is generally longer and follows a carefully prescribed format. If a vacancy announcement calls for a resume, be sure to submit a resume and not a CV, as the format may be important to the employer faced with the challenge of comparing candidates. If you are unclear as to whether a resume or CV is appropriate, contact the hiring organization to inquire. It's safer to ask the question than to gamble on the application.

What to Include in a Resume

The following model is based on a common format for a chronological resume.

Contact Information

Always put your name and contact information at the top of your resume. You want employers to be able to reach you easily if they need to ask for more information or want to schedule an interview. Be sure to include a mailing address, an email address, and at least one phone number. About that email address: Make sure it's professional (say goodbye to "beer24/7@hotmail" or "2cool4class@gmail") and reflects the kind of candidate an organization would want to hire. You may also want to include a link to a personal website, Twitter account, or LinkedIn profile in your contact information; these can be powerful ways to demonstrate your 2.0 prowess. Make sure, however, that the content on these pages is professional and appropriate. Any online information you provide is fair game for employers, so if your pages include information you wouldn't share in a workplace, don't bring them to a potential employer's attention.

Objectives or Summary of Qualifications

Many people include a statement of objectives or summary of qualifications just after their contact information on the first page of their resume. Some employers find them redundant, while others think they can add value—if done well. If you wish to include one of these on your resume, do it well. Make sure these statements add content and information; don't just restate everything the hiring committee is about to read below. Think preview, not redo. Keep objective statements or summaries of qualifications brief (two to three sentences), and emphasize keywords that tie your experience to the job requirements; for example, "An early career librarian with 5 years' experience in public services, information technology, and outreach in the sciences. Seeking career advancement and opportunities to specialize in liaison services at a larger research institution."

A word of caution here: The objective or summary statement on your resume should relate specifically to the individual position for which you are applying. As with your cover letter, you will need to tailor this statement to fit each application. If you're not willing to put in the effort to tailor your statement to fit each position, your safer bet is to leave it out entirely. Don't risk including bad information, and don't take up important real estate at the top of your resume if it fails to add value.

Education

The next section on your resume should list your educational credentials. In reverse chronological order, list each degree, the degree-granting institution, and the date your degree was conferred. If you are working on a degree, state your anticipated graduation date. If you have taken significant coursework toward a degree but have opted not to complete it at this time, you can also include that information. Limit this section to degrees achieved after high school. You may also opt to include pertinent awards or scholarship information in this section. Some applicants include their grade point average (GPA) in this section, but in our experience, this is neither necessary nor relevant.

Professional Experience

The bulk of your resume information will fall into the section on professional experience. As you progress in your career, you may need to truncate your experience to the most recent 15 years or so. At this point, change the heading to "Selected Professional Experience." You can also use this approach if you have worked outside libraries but are not including other experience in your resume.

As with your educational credentials, your professional experience should be listed in reverse chronological order, beginning with the most recent position. When describing each position, include the title of the position, the employing institution and location, the dates you held the position, and a brief description of your major responsibilities and accomplishments. Bullet points are fine as long as the content is full and descriptive. Include action verbs that show professional maturity, ownership, and responsibility. Think more along the lines of "authorized," "conducted," "assessed," and "produced," and less along the lines of "assisted" or "helped." Be sure to mind your verb tense. Use present tense for current responsibilities and past tense for responsibilities (and positions) that have ended.

It's also helpful to include size and scope notes when listing your responsibilities. Don't say "Managing a collection development budget." Instead, provide a reasonable estimate of the size of the budget, the number of account lines, and the different types of funding. For example, say something like "Managing a $800,000 collection development budget with 26 account lines on state, trust, and grant funding." Don't say "Answering questions at the reference desk." Instead, identify your clientele (students, faculty, members of the community) and the methods you use in answering their questions (in person; on the phone; via chat, instant messaging, or email). Try something like this: "Responded to reference inquiries in the physical sciences from faculty and graduate students via phone, email, and IM." Be concise, but include relevant information that will pique the reader's interest. You want to show that you have excellent written communication skills, which are being assessed along with your experience for the position.

Publications and Presentations

Next, include information about your professional research activity. As you build your career, you will build opportunities to speak or publish professionally. While professional research activity may be more common in academic libraries, continuing professional involvement is one of the keys to success for professionals in any type of library. Find the type of activity best suited to your workplace and your career stage. For entry-level librarians, these opportunities can come through in-house invitations to speak to other professionals at your home institution or at local conferences and can progress to the national speakers' circuit. Professional publication can take many forms, from publication in a peer-reviewed journal to blog postings. The key is to start looking for opportunities for publication and presentation, and be sure these activities are reflected on your resume. List a full citation of each activity, and if information is available online (conference proceedings or a link to a full-text article), include that as well. Your publications and presentations provide another way for the hiring institution to assess your communication skills and also demonstrate your commitment to and interest in the profession.

Professional Activity and Service

Along with publications and presentations, candidates should build a successful record of professional service and activity and include that record in their resume. Networking and service activities span all kinds of libraries, not just academic ones. From service on local committees or in student organizations to service in national and international organizations, your time spent working on professional issues demonstrates 1) your ability to work collegially with others, 2) strong communication and time management skills, and 3) a growing and sustained interest in the profession. Briefly list each organization, your role (such as committee member or board chair), dates of service, and major responsibilities and accomplishments during your tenure.

Professional Memberships

Indicate any professional memberships and affiliations on your resume. Include the name of the organization, dates of membership, and your role (e.g., member, director, past president). Be sure to spell out acronyms of organizations; don't assume the reader will know. If you belong to any relatively obscure organizations, you may want to include their URLs in order to enhance the reader's understanding of the group's work.

Specialized Skills

If you have specialized skills, such as expertise in a specific range of technologies or fluency in one or more foreign languages, include a section on your resume to highlight these. Be sure to also indicate your level of fluency (e.g., in bibliographic knowledge, in reading comprehension) or degree of technical knowledge.

Employment References

Although employment references and their contact information should be listed on a separate page from your resume, it is often helpful to send this information along with your cover letter and resume. (Some institutions actually require references at the time of application.) List each person's name, job title, mailing address, email address, and phone number. A brief note about a reference's professional relationship to you (e.g., supervisor, project manager, co-chair) would be helpful to the hiring supervisor or committee.

Be selective when asking someone to serve as a reference for you. Select references who will speak well on your behalf and provide a positive reference to the hiring institution. Ask people you have worked closely with, such as a current or past supervisor, a colleague at work, a colleague at another institution with whom you have worked on a project or committee, the president or chair of an organization you belong to, or a faculty member or community leader or client you have assisted as part of your job. When asking someone to serve as a reference for you, provide a copy of your resume and the vacancy announcement, and ask whether he or she will be able to provide you a positive reference related specifically to this position. Never state "References available by request" on your resume if references have already been requested in the vacancy announcement.

What *Not* to Include in a Resume

Your resume can include many different sections that highlight multiple areas of your professional life, but there are limits. In general, the following are not well received.

Photographs

This is a job application, not a modeling interview. There is absolutely no place on a resume for a personal photo of you—or of your cat.

Personal Information

This not a matchmaking service application. Unless it directly relates to the job, do not include any personal information. Employers do not care that you like kayaking, making paper airplanes, or competing in rock-climbing competitions. In very rare situations, you may have a personal interest that relates specifically to the job and may wish to mention it. (For instance, if you volunteer as a Spanish language tutor at a local elementary school, you would rightly mention this information when applying for a position as children's librarian in a library serving a predominantly Latino population.) Unless your personal interests and experiences relate to the job, however, leave them off the resume.

Whether you are married or have children is also not relevant, so do not include that information on your resume. Also do not include your Social Security number.

Precollege Employment and Education

For many, the high school years are so far away that they're hard to recall. Nonetheless, even if you can remember what you were doing during high school and have the details of all your employers during

those years, do not include this information on your resume. The
same is true for high school academic achievements, including hon-
ors, awards, or a first-place finish in your high school science fair.

GPAs and SAT/GRE Score

GPAs and SAT/GRE scores measure your ability to learn, retain,
and retrieve information during a test. Many hiring supervisors and
search committees do not consider GPAs and test scores relevant to
the practical requirements of a job, and our recommendation is not
to include this information on your resume.

Common Questions About Resumes

Following are some of the most common questions we've answered
in our columns regarding resumes:

**Q: I'm just getting started and am looking for my first profes-
sional library position. Any tips on the resume?**

First, don't undersell yourself. Be sure to highlight any experience you've had in library school, as well as transferable skills from
previous work experience during or after college. Make sure you
include student memberships, activities, and committees on your
resume. List responsibilities *and* accomplishments from your work
experience and professional activities. Look for job opportunities
that match your skills and experience. Be selective about which
positions to apply for, and put your energy into positions that best
suit your experience and interests. Seize any and all opportunities to
gain experience (paid or unpaid) and to build your expertise and
professional networks. Rely on your professional networks to learn
about positions and opportunities and to cultivate excellent employment references.

Q: I'm coming to librarianship as a second career. Is there anything special I need to do with my resume?

If you're just getting started in librarianship, you may want to consider dividing the "Professional Experience" section into two parts: "Library Experience" and "Other Related Experience." You would list your library-related experience first, in reverse chronological order, then your previous career experience under "Other Related Experience," also in reverse chronological order. Be sure to use your cover letter to highlight the transferable skills from your previous career and to make it an asset to your application. Don't forget to consider (and highlight) experience such as project management, leadership, resource allocation, supervision, or instruction and teaching. And if you have additional educational qualifications or credentials related to the previous career, include them under the "Education" section.

Q: I've been in the profession for years, and I find myself in a position to look for another opportunity. It's been a while since I've done a resume. Any advice?

If you have several years in the profession, you've probably stacked up a great deal of professional experience, service, and activity. You may want to consider adding "Selected" to the section titles on your resume, showing readers that you are including only the most recent information in these areas. If you're following the chronological resume format, your content will be listed in reverse chronological order, beginning with the most recent. In this format, you can omit the most dated content and include just the most current and relevant information. You may also want to pay special attention to the "Specialized Skills" section of your resume, making sure that your technology skills are up-to-date and accurately described.

Q: Resumes: Paper or Electronic?

Unless one format or another is specifically requested, it is generally up to the candidate to select the resume format. Many larger institutions will require all application materials to be submitted online, which requires an electronic resume and cover letter. We strongly recommend submitting your resume in PDF format so that your content and formatting will arrive as you intend. PDF is also a common platform and won't require specialized software.

If a paper resume is requested, be sure to use standard resume paper, in white or off-white (no flashy colors, no scented paper, no polka dots) and in the standard size (8.5″ x 11″ paper).

When preparing your resume for paper or electronic formats, choose a respectable, professional font in a reasonable, legible size (no less than 11-point font as a general rule). Consider how the document looks on the page. Select margins that spread the content out across the page but don't fill it up and overwhelm the reader. Make sure there are reasonable page breaks in the right places, and use bullet points to break up large sections of text.

4

ONLINE IDENTITIES: MANAGING YOUR ONLINE PRESENCE AND BUILDING YOUR BRAND

Dear Q&A: Is it really that important to have an online identity? If so, can you tell me how I can get one?

Long ago, in a time before social media sites, in a world before search engines changed the way we find and gather information, professionals didn't need to worry about what others thought of them outside the workplace—or about how people they had never met perceived their behavior, creativity, or sociability within public arenas removed from the context of their daily jobs. Professionals were judged on their work, during work hours, within the workplace, not on how they conducted or promoted themselves in online forums.

Well, times have certainly changed. We now live in a world in which people we've never met seek out information about us using search engines and social media sites. These people—potential employers, colleagues, review committees, supervisors, patrons or clients, curious admirers, even strangers—not only *expect* to find us online; they might reward us or penalize us because of what they discover. What used to be considered private or personal is now transparent and social, which means that we need to be aware of how we conduct ourselves online and be proactive in how we market ourselves online. In other words, we need to be online, and we need to be smart about it.

So, what is your online identity and why should you care? In a nutshell, your online identity is you online. Your identity is made up of whatever is findable and whatever is visible, which could be next to nothing or a plethora of different types of media (photographs, videos, comments, postings, profiles, articles, designs, reviews) or anywhere in between. It could be content that you have created or content that someone else created about you and you don't even know exists. Whatever your online identity encompasses, it is up to you to 1) discover it; 2) wrangle it into something professional; 3) develop, curate, and groom it; and 4) maintain it.

Before you begin to do all of this, you need to get over any fear you may have of putting yourself out there. Getting over that fear can be difficult. It may seem strange that you need to market yourself as an individual brand, putting information about yourself online that is open and available for the world to see. This approach may take time to get used to, and some just choose to ignore it and hope it will ignore them back. But keep in mind that there probably already is information about you online: in an online phone book or directory, on your institution's website, on an association's site or a club that you belong to or from an event that you attended, a letter you wrote to a newspaper, a review of a restaurant or a book, and so on. When you choose to create your own professional presence and monitor your online appearances, you are taking control of your own identity—and pushing to the top of the heap those things you want others to see about you.

The Importance of Branding

Tom Peters emphasized the importance of branding when he said, "Regardless of age, regardless of position, regardless of the business we happen to be in, all of us need to understand the importance of branding. We are CEOs of our own companies: Me Inc. To be in business today, our most important job is to be head marketer for the brand called You."[1]

Your Professional Online Identity

To create a professional online identity, you need to take a few steps. First, search for yourself. Pick a few different search engines, and type in your name, in quotation marks. If you have a common name, use additional keywords such as the city where you live or work, your job title, the name of your library or institution, or a nickname. You should be able to find something. If you cannot find a single thing, don't worry; this is better than finding something questionable or unprofessional.

Second, tighten up security on all your social media sites. At the very least, read the terms and privacy statements on the sites and understand what happens to the information and media you post, and who maintains ownership. Familiarize yourself with licensing and copyright terms, including Creative Commons, before you begin to create and upload content.

Third, create a professional online presence. This can be a blog, a website, an online portfolio or resume, or a profile in a professional social community. You don't need to have high-tech computer skills or web design experience to do this. It can be as simple as copying and pasting text from another document or filling out a form. There are several types of online tools, such as wikis, blogs, and easy-to-create websites, that make it simple to develop your own web presence with little or no knowledge of HTML or web design and with little or no money.

Fourth, create profiles on a variety of social media sites such as LinkedIn, Facebook, Twitter, Academia.edu, ALA Connect, and Google+, and link to your professional online presence from those profiles. These profiles can contain minimal information, such as name, job title, work history, and email address, and optional information (e.g., skills and interests, links to personal websites). Profiles such as these are easy to create and strengthen your web presence because they "live" on popular sites that have high rankings with search engines.

Once you have an online presence, or a brand, you need to use it, share it, and let people know about it. Link to it from places such as your email signature and your staff directory page. Tell your colleagues about it, and share it with your supervisor or director. Join online groups and discussions, and make yourself visible and findable online. Remember that your online presence is your brand. You need to pay attention to it, update it, and nurture it.

Self-Impression and Perception

According to Dan Schwabel, author of Me 2.0: Build a Powerful Brand to Achieve Career Success, *"To know if you've discovered your brand, you need to make this equation equal: Your self-impression = How people perceive you."*[2]

Online Portfolios

In its most basic form, an online portfolio is a resume, deconstructed and reproduced on a website. In reality, though, it can—and should—be much more. Online portfolios, like print portfolios, are used to house bodies of work and years' worth of professional materials. They are used to visually represent and showcase a productive career and are used to highlight educational and other materials to build up a budding career. Online portfolios are becoming more and more popular as a job-seeking tool (for the candidate) and as part of job application material (for the employer) because they allow hiring committees to learn more about a candidate prior to the interviewing stage.

An online portfolio is useful as

- A practical, professional-looking, and tech-savvy way to share your information with potential employers

- A convenient place to store and access your personal documents and materials

- A space that is easy to build, use, and maintain and that you can update and add to anytime, from anywhere

Here are a few tips for building and maintaining your online portfolio:

- Upload or embed only the items and documents that you own; link to ones you do not.

- Keep it organized, and think about navigation and design. Avoid long, wordy pages. You might consider creating a separate page for each section of your resume.

- Make your online portfolio visually appealing. Use images and color, and upload a professional photo of yourself.

- Include only materials that you would show your current employer.

- Make it easy for people to contact you by including brief contact information (name and email address will suffice), but do not include personal information (such as your home phone number or address). This is true for any online presence or profile.

- Use tags and keywords (if available) to help people find you via search engines.

- Be creative. Your online portfolio shouldn't be just an online replica of your resume.

- Keep it current and fresh; revise and add to it on a regular basis.

Maintaining Two Separate Online Identities

We are often asked whether a person's online identity needs to be entirely professional. What if you maintain two online personas, one for friends and one for professional purposes, one for play and one for work? Will this hurt your chances of getting hired or getting promoted? Most people who are online do have both personal and professional information, circles, contacts, and sites. People who search for you online do not expect that everything they find will be professional in nature or created specifically for professional purposes. In fact, it can be beneficial to show other sides of your personality and showcase other interests and skills and experience. It is perfectly acceptable to have nonwork, or nonprofessional, personas, sites, postings, or photos. But keep in mind that there is no online partition separating the personal from the professional—what's online is online, and nothing online is private. As with other types of information, it is up to the individual to critically evaluate what he or she finds. Remember, people's personal and professional lives are often interwoven. Many of our co-workers and colleagues are our friends, and people we meet at a party may become professional contacts, which makes it difficult (and a lot more work) to keep and maintain different sites for different groups of people.

When it comes to online identity, the line between personal and professional is very fine. Privacy online doesn't really exist—unless you are paying money for it. If you do have both a personal and a professional online persona (as many people do), make sure that your personal persona will not give anyone cause to question your judgment. Sites themselves do not determine or influence conduct, so be smart about what you put online and ask yourself, "Would I want my boss or a potential employer to see this?" Do your best to avoid inflammatory or foul language and lewd or suggestive images, and do not over-share personal or intimate information.

One good reason to have or maintain separate online identities is if you have a business that is separate from your existing professional role. In that case, you may want or need to have two separate professional identities: one for you as a librarian or professional, and one for your business.

ONLINE BRANDING

A Q&A with Lisa Chow and Sandra Sajonas of People Interact Consultancy

Q: What's your story?

We are a dynamic duo of independent information professionals who are passionate about making sense of our rapidly changing world in a way that ensures people aren't lost in the shuffle by empowering libraries and other organizations to be people-centered.

Q: Why "People Interact"?

It's about people. People interact with other people, objects, service interfaces, and so on, and that's where people-centered design comes in.

Q: How does someone get started with creating an online presence and branding?

Lisa: You can plan, plan, plan, but at some point, you just gotta do it. And that's what we did when we finally launched our online presence and branding for People Interact, after a lot of brainstorming and feedback from friends and colleagues. We know that an online presence and branding for our consultancy are important based on experiences with our individual online presences and branding. People do Google you. I've had people tell me "I Googled you" when I asked how they found out about me or found my email address. Think about who you are and what you do or what you want to be doing—make sure this comes through in your online presence and branding.

Sandra: With your online portfolio, profiles, and branding, it's important to really know yourself and the image you want to project. It is also important, when you commit to a portfolio, profile, or brand, that you are fully committed and passionate about it. It's a work in progress that you have to regularly tweak.

Q: What are your tips and advice?
- Answer the questions, *Who are you?* and *What do you do?* or *What do you want to do?*
- Just do it. You gotta start somewhere.
- Be committed. Tweak along the way.
- Ask friends and colleagues for feedback.

Personal Branding

Your online identity is your brand, or at least a large part of your brand. Before you begin creating, updating, and managing your online identity, take some time to think about what you want your brand to be and how you want to be perceived. You are in control of building your own brand, so how do you want people—potential employers, search committees, colleagues, reviewers, relatives, friends, acquaintances, your mother—to perceive you? You can highlight specific skills, experience, history, accomplishments, associations, and hobbies, and you can incorporate words and images, designs, colors, and fonts to craft your own unique mold.

So consider the following: What are your goals for building your online identity, or for creating your personal brand? Do you want to find a job? Get promoted or recognized? Build your reputation? Clean up your existing identity? Or do you simply want to gain more visibility by putting yourself out there? Your goals will help you determine what to emphasize and to make most visible, and they might determine where you choose to build profiles and how you communicate and promote yourself in online forums.

What Personal Branding Is and Is Not

On his website Career Distinction, William Arruda provides the following definition of personal branding:

Personal Branding is ...
... the process of unearthing your unique promise of value and demonstrating that value in everything you do. It's about consistently being your best self so you achieve your goals while adding tremendous value to your team, organization and company.

Personal Branding is not ...
... about creating a false image for the outside world or being self-centered or self-indulgent. It's about being your authentic self and delivering value to those around you.[3]

Having an online presence requires that you "put yourself out there." It's completely normal to be nervous about (or terrified of) this process, because it isn't something that feels natural for many of us. But if you intend to compete for jobs, promotions, recognition, or awards at some point in your career, you will need to get over that reluctance. Just jump out there, get wet, and thrash around a bit. Think of it as an exercise in self-promotion and in keeping up with technology and trends. After the initial shock, you'll get your stroke, and you'll be glad you did it.

BALANCING DUAL IDENTITIES ON THE WEB

A Q&A with Naomi House, founder, publisher, and editor of I Need a Library Job

Q: Who are you?

I launched I Need a Library Job (INALJ; inalj.com) with the help of Elizabeth Leonard in October 2010 after finding my job on a listserv. I was looking for a platform or format that I could use to share jobs with my fellow Rutgers MLIS program classmates. Since its launch, INALJ has grown by leaps and bounds. An identifiable, unique brand has been vital to growing INALJ.

Q: Why two identities?

First, decide if dual identities are truly what you need. In my case, my paying job and job duties were completely unrelated to INALJ. I work for a government contractor, so the choice was easy. I was not allowed to speak for my employer, and my employer does not specialize in library jobs. I needed an identity or brand that was independent of, though produced by, "Naomi House, MLIS."

In this day and age, when there is sure to be some measure of permanence for the digital footprints we leave, it is more important than ever to be proactive in establishing and curating your digital identities online. There are many reasons that, as a librarian or information professional, you might need or want to have separate identities on social media platforms and the wider web. It could be personal preference. It could be because your employer has strict rules about social media. It could be, as in my case, that one identity represents who you are as an individual while the other represents an organization you created.

Q: What's in a name?

When I started I Need a Library Job, I wanted the name to be something that anyone could identify with. "I" was no longer just me. "I" could be anyone who identified with needing a job or wanting a better one. "I" was really a way of saying "Me too." Later on I realized that I needed a short, easy-to-remember acronym as I Need a Library Job was too much of a mouthful, so I shortened the daily digest name to INALJ, which was also an available URL. Elizabeth, one of my classmates in the Rutgers MLIS program, set up the Facebook page and Twitter feed, and I began the daily digest.

Really think about your audience. Are you trying to get them to identify you as a resource? Are you trying to get them to see themselves as part of your group? Think about which pronouns will be appropriate. Embrace how you are perceived. I never anticipated some of the ways fans have responded, including the various pronunciations of INALJ. Go with the flow.

Q: Where?

You need to narrow down the scope of where you want to "live" on the web, and in order to decide which platforms are best, you need to sit down and think about it first. Don't rush off and create a Twitter feed or Facebook page before you decide what you will use them for and what the ground rules are. For me, Facebook and Twitter are announcement pages; my LinkedIn group is for in-depth discussions; and my website, INALJ.com, is for sharing articles and interviews and for hosting the lists of jobs resources as well as the daily INALJ Jobs Digest. Look at blogs you enjoy and whose format seems to fit, and find out what platform they use. Don't be afraid to message or email librarians who have Facebook pages, Twitter feeds, or fantastic blogs you follow for advice. Make sure you are following library-related LinkedIn groups, such as the INALJ page, and ask there as well.

Q: When?

Start thinking about it right now. You can begin by creating an elevator speech for both identities that is one sentence long each. Two sentences are not too much for a quick elevator ride. Mine is basically as follows: "I help develop and curate the library's collection of government information, and I help people find and use the historical documents. In my spare time, I like giving back to the library community by publishing a daily jobs digest with over 150–200 pages of jobs for librarians." Simple, effective, clear. It may suit you better to come up with an elevator speech that leads to more questions, so play with it. Try it out and see what responses you get.

Endnotes

1. Tom Peters, "The Brand Called You," *Fast Company*, August 31, 1997, accessed July 10, 2013, www.fastcompany.com/magazine/10/brandyou.html.
2. Dan Schawbel, "Personal Branding 101: How to Discover and Create Your Brand." *Mashable*, February 5, 2009, accessed July 10, 2013, mashable.com/2009/02/05/personal-branding-101.
3. William Arruda, "Personal Branding," *Reach Personal Branding*, n.d., accessed July 10, 2013, www.reachpersonalbranding.com/about/personal-branding.

$$Q\&A$$

5

INTERVIEWING: GETTING READY FOR THE SHOW

Dear Q&A: I finally have an INTERVIEW! I'm so excited I can barely stand it. As I get myself together, how should I prepare for the interview? What do I need to think about and what should I ask? Oh, and what on earth do I wear?

Congratulations on getting an invitation for an interview! Clearly, your impressive cover letter and resume did the job. Now nothing stands between you and the job of your dreams but the interview. Now is not the time to lose confidence in yourself or your experience.

Just remember that the purpose behind every interview is to give the hiring committee a chance to meet you (the candidate) in person, to see whether your skills and experience really match what was described on your application materials, and to see if you are a good fit with the existing personnel and organization. There are several types of interviews and different ways to prepare. However, knowing the fundamental purpose of the interview will help you keep the process in perspective. And just know that, no matter what type of institution or position you are applying for, the interview fundamentals are essentially the same. Be prepared to present yourself and your qualifications for the position in the best way possible. Knowing more about the different types of interviews and ways to prepare will position you well for success.

Types of Interviews

In general, interviews can be divided into two categories: remote interviews and in-person interviews.

Remote Interviews

Remote interviews can take a number of forms, but the most common is a telephone interview, although the use of videoconferencing via online web services such as Google Video Chat and Skype is increasing. In most cases, remote interviews are used to prescreen candidates before the hiring organization commits time and money to in-person interviews. Remote interviews can be tricky because it's hard to form a personal connection when technology stands between you and the interviewer. Candidates miss out on visual cues during a telephone call, and videoconferencing can feel impersonal. Despite these limitations, candidates can still do very well when prepared and practiced.

To practice for a telephone interview, you need to get comfortable talking to a faceless group and responding with energy and enthusiasm to the questions being asked. We recommend sitting back-to-back with a friend and responding to a set of practice interview questions. The back-to-back technique will help get you comfortable answering interview questions when you can't see the speaker's facial expressions or pick up on helpful visual cues.

Generally, telephone interviews run 30 to 60 minutes, and the questions are the same for every candidate, which means they're broad-based. (See the sidebar later in this chapter, "Commonly Asked Interview Questions You Should Be Prepared to Answer.") Preparing for a telephone interview is very similar to preparing for an in-person interview. You should know how your skills and experiences match the qualifications and responsibilities of the job. Candidates should be prepared to talk about their professional interests, especially as they relate to the position. Candidates should respond to behavior-based questions ("Tell us about a time when you ...") with specific examples of projects and experiences.

In addition to the basic interview prep, candidates should be prepared at the time of the call. Be in a quiet space where you won't be disturbed or distracted. Have your interview materials set out in front of you, as well as a copy of the vacancy announcement. Dress for an interview and sit at a table or desk during the call in order to help yourself feel more professional and sound more engaged than if you were reclining on the sofa in your pajamas. Sitting at a desk or table will allow you to have all the necessary materials organized in front of you, and the interviewer(s) won't have to listen to the shuffling of papers as you look for specific notes and documents.

Dressing the part and preparing for the interview rise to a whole new level if you're planning for a videoconference interview. You will be not only heard but also seen, and so will your desk and surrounding environment. Find an appropriate space to conduct your video interview, which means a neat, clean, private, quiet space with good lighting.

At the conclusion of a telephone or video interview, be sure to send a simple note to say thank you for the time and opportunity. Do so by both email and snail mail (more on this later). Make your note a genuine expression of your appreciation, as well as an invitation to talk further about the position.

In-Person Interviews

In-person interviews vary in format and can range from a couple of hours to a full day or longer. In some cases, you may meet with one or two people from the organization; in others, you may interview with a panel of representatives or meet with scores of people during one-on-one and large-group meetings throughout the day. An in-person interview usually requires more preparation than a phone interview does because the experience is longer, the questions are deeper and more detailed, and the candidate may be required to make a presentation.

Be prepared to meet a lot of people and to answer the same questions over and over again, because each time there will be someone new in the audience. If it feels awkward saying the same thing over again, focus directly on the person in the room you haven't met yet, and answer the question as if he or she has asked it.

Remember to listen as much as you talk and to take in everything about the experience. While it's hard not to think of yourself as the one in the hot seat, you are interviewing the interviewers as much as they are interviewing you. Be mindful of how people interact with each other. How do you perceive their conversations? Are they friendly with one another? Is there good energy in the room? Do people seem engaged and happy to be at work? Are you picking up on negative vibes that you might want to explore with the supervisor? How do people describe their work? How do they describe the library? How do they describe the library's role within the school/university/company/community?

Make notes about the people you meet during the interview, especially if you've had a great conversation about a mutual interest or if a particular person has been very helpful throughout the day. This information will really help with your post-interview thank-you notes. Record your thoughts, questions, and impressions of meetings throughout the day.

Commonly Asked Interview Questions You Should Be Prepared to Answer

- *Tell us about your interest in this position.*
- *Tell us about your experience as it relates to this position.*
- *Tell us about a time when you provided excellent public service.*
- *Describe a project you worked on with others. What was your role on the project, and how did you support the work of the group?*
- *This position requires someone who can juggle a lot of responsibilities. Tell us about a time when you had to manage a number of priorities. How did you decide what came first, and how did you meet all the deadlines?*
- *Please describe your experience and comfort level with technology. Can you give us an example of a project you worked on that required specific technical skills?*
- *Tell us about a time when something didn't go as planned. How did you respond and what actions did you take?*
- *Where do you see yourself in the next 2 to 3 years?*
- *Do you have any questions for us?*

How to Prepare for an Interview

The Basics

Preparation is always the key to success. Your preparation for an interview actually starts with tailoring your application materials to the job announcement. In your cover letter and resume, you've already stated why you are an excellent candidate for the position. Use this groundwork to also prepare for the interview. Study the job announcement, cover letter, and resume, and review the reasons you are a great fit for the job. Have these materials with you during any type of interview, remote or in person, and underline relevant parts to remind yourself of key strengths you bring to the position.

If you receive an interview packet or other information from the hiring institution, study everything in it. The institution is providing this material for a reason. Take some additional time to study the organization's web presence. As we discussed in the previous chapter, online branding is a powerful thing, and organizations use their online materials to develop a personal brand and identity, just as individuals do. By examining the organization's web presence, you can get a feel for the kind of organization it is or aspires to be. Locate information about the specific department, library, and parent institution, as well as about the community and surrounding areas.

If you have the opportunity to visit the location before the actual day of the interview, do so. Walk around, take a look at the facilities, feel what it's like to be a visitor, and then incorporate this experience into your comments and replies during the interview. Make sure you've seen an organizational chart and read the strategic plan, the library's annual report, and its mission, vision, or values statement. Find circulation statistics and gate counts, if published. Identify the role and research specialties of the individuals with whom you are meeting throughout the day. Try to put together a complete picture of the organization you're walking into so that you can place the library, and the job, in context.

Don't forget that you are interviewing them, too. Have questions prepared to ask throughout the day as you meet with different individuals and groups. Ask about the work itself and performance expectations, as well as organizational issues, including management structure, reporting relationships, and cultural norms and values.

Interview Prep Checklist: Things to Take With You

- *Job announcement*
- *Cover letter, resume, and list of references*
- *STAR grid (discussed later) with specific examples*
- *Notebook and pen*
- *Portfolio with extra printed materials (just in case) that you've created or worked on (e.g., articles, thesis, websites, design work, newsletters)*
- *Interview materials included in interview packet (e.g., travel information, interview schedule, organizational chart, strategic planning documents, map, floor plan)*
- *Water bottle, tissues, and mints*
- *Brush, comb, and other accoutrements (e.g., lipstick, lip balm, hairspray, extra pair of tights or pantyhose, anti-static spray)*
- *Briefcase or professional-looking bag for carrying all of the aforementioned materials*

Answering Behavior-Based Questions

You'll need to be prepared to answer a lot of questions, most of which will be behavior-based and designed to elicit relevant details. If an interviewer asks whether you have public service experience, a simple yes or no answer won't be very helpful to either of you. If, instead, you provide examples, the interviewer will not just learn that you have experience but will gain an appreciation for how you define and apply excellent public service.

The most difficult part of preparing for behavior-based questions is thinking of specific situations on demand. You might not think it would be all that hard to draw from your own personal experience, but in the throes of an interview situation, a lot can slip your mind. That's why we like to recommend preparing with the Situation, Task, Action, Result (STAR) model.

STAR Model

Situation	Task	Action	Result
Experience 1			
Experience 2			

When preparing for your interview, map out several scenarios from your previous experience that either relate to the primary functions of the position (e.g., public service, web design, project management, grant writing) or demonstrate some of the desired characteristics of the successful candidate (e.g., innovation, creativity, collaboration, enthusiasm, service orientation). Create a grid of your personal experiences, and fill in the STAR categories for each situation. When preparing for your interview, study these experiences, analyze the STAR categories, and be prepared to discuss these examples with others. Be sure to bring the grid to your interview in case you need to refer to it throughout the day.

You can also use the STAR model to prepare for interview questions that relate to how you might do something differently in the future. We all dread the question, "What's your biggest failure?" during an interview. While we personally wish this question would never be asked, you should be prepared with an answer—because the only thing worse than having to answer this question is not being *able* to answer it. Using the STAR model, think about a situation or task and how the action you took did not result in a desired outcome. This situation is your example.

But don't stop there! You don't want to end on a note of failure, so add an additional end to the story: Provide an alternative action and an alternative result to demonstrate how you could approach this situation differently in the future. Then the story ends, not with failure, but with self-reflection, thoughtfulness, and an action plan for future success.

What to Wear

It's always the same question. What do I wear to the interview? For men, a suit or sport coat? Maybe a sweater vest and tie? For women, a pantsuit or a skirt? Stockings? What about a sweater set?

Just know that for the interview, you will most likely be the best-dressed person in the room—and that is OK. Be sure to project a neat, clean, professional image. Your clothes should be tailored to fit, neither baggy nor too tight. While it should go without saying, ladies, make sure everything is covered—in other words, wear nothing too revealing.

Shoes should be clean and appropriate. Don't wear sneakers, sandals, or flip-flops (even your fancy ones). A general rule is that your shoes should be a shade darker than your pants, so no white shoes with black pants.

Accessories should not be a distraction. If your big hoop earrings jingle when you move your head, or your bracelets clank every time you shake hands, you're going to have a long day ahead of you.

The basic rules of thumb: A man should wear a suit or a sport coat with dress slacks, a dress shirt, tie, and dress shoes. A woman should wear a pantsuit, a jacket and dress skirt, or a professional-looking skirt and sweater set; skirts should be below the knee, with either stockings or tights. Hair, makeup, and jewelry should be conservative.

What to Expect From the Organization

When you've been invited to interview with an organization, you can expect some basic information. You should be given a date, time, and location for the interview. If your interview is in another state, you should receive information about travel plans (airline and hotel confirmation numbers, rental car arrangements, etc.) if the organization is making the arrangements for you. If travel arrangements aren't mentioned, ask whether you will be reimbursed for your travel expenses.

You should also expect to receive information about the interview itself, such as an interview schedule; the names and titles of the individuals with whom you will meet; whether you are expected to make a presentation, and if so, the topic, expected duration, intended audience, and any technical requirements. In addition, you may receive basic information about the organization, including an organizational chart, a strategic plan, and a recent copy of the annual statistics. If there are basic governance documents for promotion or tenure, these should be included. Some organizations also include information on the community as part of an interview packet. If any of these items are not included, ask the institution to send this information to you, if possible, as you prepare.

Concluding Your Interview

Congratulations for having made it through the interview process! Relax, and reflect on what went well and how you might improve next time. And be prepared to wait for further word—it could be as long as several weeks before you hear from the institution. There will be large pools of candidates for some library positions, and numerous people may be expected to provide feedback. Other times, city or county government human resource offices handle the recruitment, and they may take a while to certify the selected candidate. Be patient. Wait 2 or 3 weeks, and then email or call to check on the status of the search.

Remember to write thank-you notes. While email supports ongoing communication, a handwritten thank-you card sent by snail mail may help you stand out. In just three or four sentences, you can genuinely express your appreciation and gratitude to the people who made the interview day possible and—dare we say—pleasant. Don't miss this simple opportunity to make a great impression.

INTERVIEWING

A Q&A with Laura Blessing, director of personnel management at North Carolina State University Libraries

Q: What typically happens during an interview?

Interviews for librarian jobs vary widely. Some consist only of an hour-long session with a supervisor while others last a day or more and require meetings with the search committee, the library director, and various other employees throughout the library. Some interviews require that candidates give a presentation. Once offered an interview, make sure you are clear on what exactly is required.

Q: How do I prepare for an interview?

First, do your research. Find out what the library's mission and goals are as well as any major upcoming issues (e.g., are they renovating the library building, opening a new branch, dealing with budget cuts). Mention these details when answering various interview questions to show that you understand the library's issues. Also research standard interview questions and have answers prepared. Most books and websites on interviewing contain examples of frequently asked interview questions and guides to answering them.

Second, know your past achievements. Write down previous successes that have occurred during library school or in the workplace. Practice integrating these stories of achievements into your answers to standard interview questions.

And, finally, don't just prepare answers, prepare questions. Prepare questions beforehand that are tailored toward each group of individuals you will meet. Also, listen carefully when they speak during the interview so you have follow-up questions to their statements, as well.

Q: What if I am asked a question I'm unable to answer?

It's OK to admit that you do not know the answer to a given question. If possible, however, try to answer as much of the question as you can (e.g., "I can't speak to the first part of the question, but as for the second part ..."). Otherwise, answer all questions as directly as possible.

Q: What should I wear for an interview?

It's never wrong to wear a suit. If you're able to afford a traditional, neutral-colored suit that fits you well, that may be your best bet. Keep in mind that your interviewers will assume that you are dressed your absolute best on your interview day. If a suit is outside your budget, do your best to find an outfit that is professional-looking. Consult catalogs from clothing stores that offer business attire to get ideas about what is appropriate. With your suit, don't forget to wear comfortable but professional-looking shoes and keep jewelry to a minimum.

Q: How do I ask about salary?

This is probably the trickiest question because there is such variety in how flexible libraries are able to be in this area. Do as much research on this as possible before the interview. Public libraries and libraries at public universities may, for example, be required to post salaries of their employees. This will give you a good idea of salary ranges for the type of job you want. Also, current or former employees may have insider information about compensation practices in that library. Finally, questions about compensation are best brought up with an appropriate individual (e.g., the human resources officer for the library or the library's director) rather than as part of a group meeting.

Q: What do I do after the interview?

Send thank-you notes. These can be either traditional paper thank-you notes or thank-you emails. Some libraries may prefer paper, but this seems to be changing rapidly. At a minimum, send thank-you notes to the highest-level person you interviewed with (the director, for example), the supervisor of the position, and anyone you had a one-on-one meeting with. It's also nice to send thank-you notes to administrative assistants who helped with your travel arrangements and to anyone else who worked to make your interview day a success.

Q: How long will it be before I know anything?

For various reasons, a library search can take many months. You can ask about the timeline of the search during your interview. If you haven't heard anything from the library a few weeks after the final candidate interviewed, it's reasonable to call and ask for an update.

Part Two
Staging Your
Own Set

"At times in my life, the only place I have been happy is when I am on stage."

—Bob Dylan

6

NETWORKING: GETTING INVOLVED IN THE PROFESSION

Dear Q&A: I've been a member of my state professional association for a few years now and have been invited to participate in a membership-level committee. I think it's a good idea to accept, but I just want to be sure I know what I'm getting into.

There are many reasons for seeking and accepting opportunities for professional involvement. In some libraries, professional service is a requirement for promotion or tenure. In others, library directors like to see their employees actively representing the library on the local, state, or national stage. And librarians may just want to (or need to) be involved with like-minded individuals, groups, committees, and associations that can provide a community of support, an external knowledge base, and an alternative outlet for professional communication. No matter what type of library you work in or what type of pressure you may have (or not have) to seek professional involvement, it's wise—and beneficial to your career—to keep current with local, state, national, and international trends; to build a greater network of colleagues; and to contribute to the professional conversation beyond your day job.

Professional service and activity opportunities take many shapes and forms, with something for everyone.

Active Involvement in Associations

Max Messmer, CEO of Robert Half International, commented about the importance of involvement in the July 2005 issue of Strategic Finance: *"Active involvement with associations can boost your visibility in the community and with your employer by showing how serious you are about your work and professional development. Take the time to select groups that align with your interests and priorities and look for ways to maximize your membership. An enhanced role with professional organizations may be just what you need to accelerate your career and move closer to achieving your goals."[1]*

Local Organizations

Local organizations provide a nice point of entry for a new librarian, a librarian who doesn't have funding to attend national conferences or doesn't want to (or cannot) travel, or a librarian who is seeking ways to get more involved. You'll usually see familiar faces, making it less frightening to walk into a local meeting or conference. You are instantly connected to the people you meet because you share a geographic locale, and you might just become friends and collaborators with colleagues at local institutions. With local organizations, the travel expenses associated with meetings, conference attendance, and programming tend to be much lower than with regional or national involvement. Additionally, local service helps you feel as if you're making a difference in your own backyard. If you're motivated and have good ideas, your local experience will be a jumping-off point for leadership roles and more national involvement down the road; as the famous quote says, "The reward for work well done is the opportunity to do more."[2] Explore the various local organizations in your area, and inquire about board membership or ways to volunteer or get involved. If you are extra motivated, start your own local organization or informal group (roundtable, meetup, discussion group, happy hour, etc.).

Statewide Organizations

State organizations can provide many of the same benefits as local ones: familiar faces, a focus on issues affecting your area, and community service opportunities. However, the scope of these types of associations is broader, and they will encompass a wider variety of institutions. Statewide library associations generally represent many types of libraries and typically hold annual meetings or conferences to discuss the issues and trends associated with libraries and other cultural institutions throughout the state. These associations bring together library professionals from a variety of backgrounds, with a common thread of state issues, budgets, politics, and geography.

National and International Organizations

Membership and service in national and international organizations are fantastic ways to shape the professional conversation and agenda. These organizations give you the opportunity to meet leaders of the profession and talk about current and future issues and trends in libraries. National and international organizations can be quite large, with thousands of members and dozens of committees, activities, and initiatives. Professional involvement at this level requires a larger time and monetary commitment, so be sure that you are willing and able to travel and attend national or international meetings (and that your institution is supportive). It may at first be challenging (and perhaps a bit overwhelming) as you find your way, learn to focus on what appeals to you, and figure out where you belong. Just remember, though, everyone was new at one point. In a few years, you'll be the expert, and someone new will be seeking your assistance in navigating such a large organization.

PROFESSIONAL INVOLVEMENT

Billy Cook, 2012 MLS graduate of the School of Information and Library Science (SILS) at the University of North Carolina (UNC) at Chapel Hill

Since library science is a professional degree, I knew going into the graduate program that my primary goals were to create a network and strengthen my resume. Any activities that supported these objectives became my top priority. Active involvement in professional organizations and memberships was one of the most important ways I was able to accomplish my goals and place myself in a strong position for employment.

Following are five tips for getting started with professional organizations.

1. Start early and start local. It's never too early to start networking and getting involved. Even before the first semester began, I had introduced myself to current and fellow incoming students via email and Facebook and started attending functions hosted by the SILS. Once the semester began, I joined the

Librarians' Association at UNC–Chapel Hill (LAUNC-CH), an organization that provides valuable programs without the added costs of travel or expensive membership.

2. Attend information sessions sponsored by student chapters. At UNC–Chapel Hill, we have several student organizations, including chapters of the American Library Association (ALA), Special Libraries Association (SLA), and Society of American Archivists. I had no idea what area of librarianship I was interested in or what the benefits of membership are, so I attended all their information sessions. This was a great way not only to get information but also to network with fellow students, local librarians, and members from the state division. Plus, these sessions often feature free food and membership giveaways, and you can't go wrong with that.

3. Join an organization and become a student leader. Even after the information sessions, I still had only a vague idea of my interests, so I joined ALA and SLA. Together they cover a large portion of librarianship and offer great benefits, and the student membership prices are unbeatable. Later that year, we held elections for new student organization leaders. I was nominated and elected president of the student chapter of SLA and community development chair (social chair) for the SILS-specific student organization. Although I didn't know it at the time, accepting these posts was one of the best decisions I made as a student. Involvement in these organizations strengthened my leadership skills, enhanced my resume, and made my time in library school a lot more fun.

4. Collaborate. Once you become involved in student organizations, you are limited only by your creativity when it comes to programming. There's nothing to prevent you from collaborating with state divisions, different student groups, students in other schools, or the local community. For example, the UNC SLA chapter was awarded the 2011 Certificate of Merit in Innovative

Programming, in part for facilitating the creation of a circulating library for the Orange County Rape Crisis Center (OCRCC). The project came to the attention of the SLA chapter when an administrator at the OCRCC expressed the center's need on the school listserv. Because of the enormity of the project, our group enlisted the help of the UNC Student Chapter of the ALA to pool resources and broadcast the importance of the project to the community. Within 2 months, our team was able to create a database to manage holdings and provide the OCRCC with an annotated list of reference materials to purchase. In addition, I leveraged my position as SILS social chair to host a happy hour fundraiser in support of this project, and with the help of students and the local community, we raised almost $300 toward the purchase of new materials.

5. Attend conferences. Continuous professional development is a vital part of librarianship, and attending conferences is an easy way to keep up with new trends and fill in any gaps in your MLS program. My first conference was the LAUNC-CH annual meeting, and it was a great way to gain experience before braving events as massive as ALA and SLA annual meetings. Going to conferences also opens doors for involvement at the national and international level. While you are there, sit in on business meetings, introduce yourself to committee members, and offer to volunteer.

All the activities just outlined are great ways to expand your professional network. The most fruitful internships and job leads came from people I had worked with or met through professional organizations.

How to Get Involved

Within all of these organizations, there is a role for everyone. If you prefer to work alone on projects, you might want to consider serving as webmaster or volunteer coordinator for a committee or section of the organization such as a discussion group. If your preference is to work with others, look for opportunities to serve on committees, task forces, or working groups within the organization. When starting out, attend a few different meetings to explore what's available. Then, once you've found an opportunity that matches an interest, find ways to serve. Most organizations (local, state, national, and international) have an appointment process for matching volunteers to positions. Find out more about that process and the timeline, and get yourself involved.

Benefits of Professional Involvement

There are many benefits of professional involvement. Most professional organizations couldn't function without the work of volunteers, and you have the opportunity to make a difference through your efforts. In return for what you provide the organization, you are rewarded with professional networks, leadership opportunities, and the ability to shape the professional agenda and contribute to the professional conversation. Your involvement, service, and activity may also have an impact on the promotion or tenure process within your library.

Another benefit of professional involvement is your growth as a professional. You will learn about other organizations and from other librarians. You will have opportunities to move into and experience new roles, and you will be building up your resume and connecting with potential employers, colleagues, and collaborators. By going outside your workplace and engaging in the larger profession, you are becoming known and getting noticed. And you never know what bigger and better things may lie ahead.

What to Do at Your First Conference or Professional Meeting

Not sure what to do now that you're finally attending your first conference? Here are a few tips:

- *Find a mentor or someone who can walk you through your first meeting.*
- *Get organized and map out a plan; study the agenda carefully.*
- *Be prepared to introduce yourself and briefly describe what you do at work and your role at the conference; have your elevator speech ready to share.*
- *Be friendly, professional, and polite.*
- *Look for opportunities to get involved, but don't overcommit; you want a reputation as someone who gets stuff done, not as someone who takes on responsibility but doesn't follow through.*
- *Bring business cards to share with new acquaintances, and collect business cards from others; this exchange is an important part of building your network.*
- *Dress professionally, but in comfortable clothing and shoes.*
- *Take notes. Jot down ideas and questions and interesting tidbits. Write down URLs and names and titles of presentations so you can look them up later. Think about ways to use this information at your library, in your job, and at your local organization.*

> • *Follow up and follow through! After the conference, allow time to reflect on your experience. What did you enjoy? What would you do differently? Which meetings made the most impact, and why? How can you get more involved? In what ways can you contribute next time? With whom do you need to follow up in terms of completing a conversation or asking for more information? How will you share your experiences with co-workers at your home institution?*

While all of this professional involvement comes with a price, we prefer to think of it as an investment. Not all organizations can fund (in whole or in part) professional development expenses for employees. Many institutions see it as a shared expense because both the employee and the employer benefit. Be prepared to invest your time and expertise, and some of your own money, in professional activities and conferences in order to build and enhance your career. Many conferences now offer online components for attendees, presenters, and volunteers—especially helpful for those who cannot afford or are unable to travel. Also, look into sharing travel and conference expenses with colleagues or friends.

Finally, remember that this is work. When you volunteer to lead a committee, administer a listserv, edit a webpage, or coordinate volunteers, you are signing up for extra work outside of the regular responsibilities of your day-to-day position. Be sure to budget your time accordingly. Take on only those responsibilities you can actually commit to seeing to completion. Your early successes in delivering a solid final product on time will grow into a national reputation as a trustworthy colleague.

THE IMPORTANCE OF NETWORKING AND GETTING INVOLVED

Caroline Fuchs, associate professor and outreach librarian at St. John's University, New York, NY

As an academic librarian, I recognize that I am in the fortunate position of having the opportunity to play a vital role in academia and in helping to determine the direction of higher education. Yet I am keenly aware that one librarian in one institution can do little to effect change. Or can she?

To succeed as librarians, we need to understand that we are members of a community, both within and outside of our own institutions. Our work is not really about resources. It's about making connections. Library resources do not in themselves provide a particularly efficacious service without the skilled assistance of a librarian. But our role goes beyond that: Librarians who do not network with colleagues or who are not involved with professional organizations are missing out.

I can't emphasize enough the importance of getting involved with professional organizations. First, join a library organization. I strongly encourage all librarians to be active members of national and local professional organizations such as ALA, SLA, or the Association of College and Research Libraries (ACRL). But it is just as important to become active in regional or state groups as well. It is in those more localized groups that opportunity often arises for leadership positions. Second, step up your membership by volunteering to serve on committees or helping out at an event. National organizations call for volunteers annually (check out their websites). Sometimes the volunteer process is more simplified for local organizations, and participation may require less travel and expense. Successful volunteer and committee work here may later prove to be an entry point for a national committee appointment.

Third, attendance at professional conferences and events, national or local, is a fine way to become more involved in the profession without the formalized commitment associated with committee work. At these functions, you can attend lectures, workshops, discussions, and roundtables, which will not only keep you current in the field but also enable you to discover future trends.

Informally, just meeting at these events with librarians from a variety of institutions who have a variety of different specializations can revitalize and invigorate your own professional development. These events also enable you to talk with others who may be in situations similar to yours, as well as librarians with more experience than you. They can be the perfect forum in which to develop a collegial support system within your field and your specialization.

So how did I get started? I became involved in my local ACRL chapter by volunteering for our annual symposium planning committee, where I developed close collegial relationships with other committee members. From there I was appointed to the chapter's executive board as the organization's legislative liaison, which further broadened my professional network. This position in turn enabled me to attend the annual National Library Legislative Day in Washington, DC, where I was able to meet and work with librarians from throughout my state and across a variety of library types (public, academic, school, etc.) while at the same time joining forces with librarians from across the U.S. Within a few years, I was elected vice president and president-elect of my local chapter. With a professional colleague, I answered the call-for-volunteers from a regional library group. I now co-chair two special-interest groups for this organization. During this same time, I volunteered to serve on ACRL and Reference and User Services Association committees. I've been appointed to several in both divisions and am currently co-chair of the American Federation of Labor, Congress of Industrial Organizations, and ALA Joint Committee on Library Services to Labor Groups. Because appointments to national committees require attendance at the ALA midwinter and annual conferences, while there I attend the ACRL chapter council meetings, to which I was elected secretary for 2013.

While all this committee work makes me extremely busy, the professional rewards and personal satisfaction derived from my involvement in these library organizations is beyond measure. I have been able to build a network of professional support and friendship that extends way beyond the walls of my institution. The librarians I have met along the way have inspired and encouraged me, which in turn rejuvenates me as a professional. Their collegiality is immeasurable; their friendships, priceless.

Endnotes

1. Max Messmer, "Counting the Benefits of Association Involvement," *Strategic Finance*, July 2005, pp. 12–14.
2. "Jonas Salk," *Wikiquote*, accessed July 10, 2013, en.wikiquote.org/wiki/Jonas_ Salk.

7

FROM HERE TO THERE: TIME FOR A CHANGE

Dear Q&A: I've been in my first professional position for about 4 years now, and I'm starting to think it's time for a change. What should my first step be?

When it's time for a change, there are several steps to planning a graceful exit and graceful re-entry. It's helpful to know where you're going, so you need to start out with a plan.

Whether you've had a lot of success in a position, or you know it's just time to move on to something different, you may find it is easier to move from one position to another than it was to secure your first job. In some cases, your position may change and grow with you, while in others, you'll move up within the same organization. In other cases, you may need to leave the organization entirely to experience the professional growth or transition that you are seeking. In any of these situations, it's important that you know what you're looking for in a position. It's also important for you to be able to articulate your professional interests and needs, as well as your strengths, talents, and abilities.

First, it is important to recognize certain differences between moving internally and moving externally. Moving up within an organization presents challenges that are different from those of moving to a higher-level position at a different institution. In some cases, you may retain responsibility for some of your former duties in addition to those that accompany your new role. In other cases, you may be filling an entirely different position, in which case you'll need to work with colleagues in new and different ways. Changing their perception from the current you to the "new you" can be a challenge and may require some time and attention. This change will be more difficult if you are moving from being a peer to being a manager. (You'll find more on this in Chapter 11.)

Moving to a position in a different organization is in many ways like starting over, including all the positives and negatives of a new start. It can be hard to start anew—making new connections with colleagues, learning a new job and a new place, getting settled, and feeling comfortable and prepared—but it can also be exciting. You have the opportunity to build on previous experience, create something new and different, and build broader professional connections and networks.

MOVING ACROSS THE COUNTRY FOR A NEW JOB

Jennifer L. Ward, information technology services employee at University of Washington Libraries

Just do it! Those three words are not just a Nike slogan or a mantra that my colleague repeats when we're being slow with some aspect of a systems implementation. It's also something you can tell yourself if you're hesitating about moving to an unfamiliar city for a job.

Perhaps you've already come to realize this, but you can do anything for 2 years. That's long enough to give everything new in your life (job, house, friends, etc.) a chance to settle down and for you to determine whether it's a good fit. If it's not, then you can move on. In the meantime, you've gained work experience and have strengthened your professional network, you know exactly how many boxes of books you really feel like packing and unpacking again, and you have hopefully had some great experiences in your new town. With a couple of years of work experience under your belt, more, different, and/or better opportunities might be available in a location that's more appealing to you. On the other hand, over 2 years, you may be slowly be realizing that this previously unfamiliar place you never thought you'd move to is home, and you can't easily imagine yourself living anywhere else.

My own career path began in North Carolina, with a brief stop in Illinois for graduate school, then on to Seattle. I'd never been to Illinois prior to grad school but chose to leave familiar ground because I wanted to travel a bit and figured that I could do anything (in this case, live in Illinois) for a year. A fantastic professional opportunity came my way midway through that first year, so 1 year of graduate school stretched into 2. During that time, I met great people who are still close friends and colleagues, learned a lot, and realized that I am not a huge fan of seemingly endless snowy winters.

After graduation, I was fortunate to receive two comparable job offers, one in North Carolina and the other in Seattle. I recall two incidents from the year before that indicated that Seattle might not be right for me, even though I'd never visited the Pacific Northwest. First, I had remarked earlier that winter (after gloomy-weather-in-Illinois day No. 3) that I couldn't move to

Seattle, as the gray would drive me crazy. Then, during my second year in Illinois, I sublet an apartment from someone who had just moved to Seattle, and he said rents there were easily double what they were in central Illinois. With these experiences in mind, I carefully considered whether I should return to my home state or move to the other side of the country, where I knew absolutely no one, and to a city that had, in my mind, a couple of strikes against it.

In the end, I took the job in Seattle. I'd just proven experimentally that I could do anything for 2 years, and this was a 2-year internship opportunity. If the gloomy weather and rain got to me, if I missed my family too much, if I didn't make any friends, if it didn't work out, I'd know for sure that Seattle didn't suit me. At the very least, I'd get that first job onto my resume, live in a different city, and explore a part of the country I'd not seen before.

Fortunately, the gamble paid off. My job is still challenging and ever-changing, and my co-workers are engaged in their work and good people to work with. Twelve years on, I still think Seattle is a great place to live. (Months of gloomy days are offset by strategically timed trips to sunny locations.) Family and friends wonder if I'll ever move east, and at some point I probably will, but I'm not quite ready yet. For now, I'm glad I had the courage to take a giant leap into the unknown. What do you have to lose? Just do it!

Getting Ready

When it's time to start looking for a new opportunity, there are several things you need to consider. First, are you looking for new opportunities within the same organization? If so, then have a conversation with your supervisor, mentor, or other trusted colleagues to identify possible opportunities (both formal and informal) on the horizon. If you are seeking new opportunities outside your current organization, decide whether you will tell others, and particularly your immediate supervisor, that you're looking. Librarianship is a very small profession with a lot of professional connections, so unless you are very, very discreet and request confidentiality throughout the search process, it is likely that someone will find out you're looking. Be sure to manage this situation as well as possible, which might include having a confidential conversation with your supervisor about being on the market.

Whether internal or external, you'll want to prepare yourself to take advantage of new opportunities. Consider taking on additional leadership tasks, enrolling in management and supervisory training, and updating your resume.

Moving From One Field of Librarianship to Another

It can be difficult to move from one field of librarianship to another. Libraries share some common traits, of course, but each is unique in terms of clientele, collection, and culture. When applying for a job that will take you in a new direction, besides highlighting your specific library experience, use your application materials (cover letter, resume, and references) to emphasize transferable skills (i.e., skills you've learned in one context that will serve you well in another). Be sure your cover letter expresses a deep interest in and enthusiasm for the position, and draw parallels between your experience and the needs of the position. Your resume should do the same by highlighting the experience and accomplishments that relate to your current and previous positions as well as to the position you are applying for. Finally, use your references wisely. Be sure to let them know you are applying for a position outside your current field of librarianship and ask whether there's anything you can provide that will prepare them to speak about your adaptability.

Additionally, think broadly about your professional network. Have you met new folks through your service in professional organizations? Worked with someone on an association project? One major benefit of your experience in professional organizations lies in expanding your professional network of folks who do similar work in all sorts of different organizations. The networks you build through your professional involvement can benefit you in important ways as you embark on the job search process; they can, for example, help you identify new positions and find professional references.

In your application materials, talk about the core values and responsibilities of libraries—collection building, access, facilities, technology, instruction and research assistance, and connecting with a constituency—all of which are relevant regardless of setting (e.g., in school libraries and public libraries). Be careful to avoid basing your comments on assumptions. Instead, base them on data gathered via research and experience in different types of libraries. For example, it's not generally well received when someone external to the operation makes a "Sure, I could do that" statement without any experience to back it up. Tread carefully with comments and assumptions such as "the only difference between school and public libraries is the clientele." There will be many other differences, ranging from funding to collections, to access, and to responsibilities. So enter the search process with confidence in your experience but also with an intellectual curiosity to explore those differences.

It is always the candidate's responsibility to "sell" his or her candidacy to the hiring institution. When you are thinking of switching fields, look at your current and previous experience and draw parallels between what you've done and what the hiring institution is looking for. Try to put things into a context and a vocabulary that are similar. For example, if you are interested in moving from a school library to a public services position in an academic library, talk about the reference assistance and instruction you provide, one-on-

one and in small and large groups. Emphasize your research consultations with upper-level students and how you assist with the research process. Highlight your experience working with teaching faculty and instructors.

THE CHANGING FIELDS OF LIBRARIANSHIP

Suzanne Crow, library director at The Spence School, New York, NY

When I decided to become a librarian, I did so with the very deliberate intention of pursuing the academic track. After I completed my information science graduate work, I was thrilled to be offered an entry-level job in a university library in New York City. After 2 years learning the ropes in that position and shedding my mantle of inexperience, I moved on to a wonderful job in an academic medical library. I stayed in that position for 8 years, and during that time I gained valuable experience in reference, library instruction, and collection development and developed fantastic collegial relationships. The work was everything that I hoped for. I loved collaborating with graduate and medical students, and the work provided one satisfying challenge after another.

While I loved the work and adored my colleagues, my personal life was beginning to tug at my sleeve—literally! I had two children within a few years, and, slowly, the careful balance between motherhood and librarianship began to feel a little too wobbly. It seemed to be time for a change.

I never considered leaving librarianship—I loved it too much to leave it. But I did want to work in a job that would allow me to find a new balance. My mother had been a school librarian for many years, and she inspired me to investigate that track. The more I learned, the more I realized that school librarianship would fit my interests perfectly. I worried, however, that I would never have a shot at such a position, particularly since my professional experience had been exclusively in academic libraries.

I began to educate myself in the field. I set up informational interviews with school librarians, did a great deal of reading, and enrolled in an online course in young adult literature. This served both to educate me and to demonstrate to my future employer my commitment to school librarianship (despite my lack of school experience).

When I learned that there was a library director position open at the Spence School, I was excited to apply and then over the moon to be offered the position. I have now completed my third year at Spence, and the job is far and away the most rewarding of my career. I get to work with amazing teachers, supportive administrators, and smart and energetic fifth- through 12th-grade girls every day. I feel privileged to teach my students the building blocks of information literacy, and I can't wait to get to school every day. The best part of the new job is that I had no idea how much I would love it. Icing on the cake is that the school schedule closely matches my family's needs. I feel very lucky to have successfully made the shift.

Creative Ideas for Getting From Here to There

Moving from one position or one library to another can be easier said than done. You may need to get creative to make it happen, and sometimes that means taking a step sideways in order to eventually move forward. Perhaps you're a cataloging librarian in an academic library, but you want to work in a public library as a reference librarian. It may be difficult to move directly into your dream job, but you might consider first moving into a cataloging position in a public library. Once established in your public library cataloging position, you can begin to take on some reference desk hours or serve at a public service point. Perhaps you are an information technology (IT) person in a large public library, looking to work in an academic library IT department. As an intermediate step, you might want to consider moving to a community college library or a small academic library, which would allow you to gain valuable experience and a sense of the type of work and clientele. Remember, a sideways step is still a step closer to your end goal.

Another way to get some valuable experience is to accept volunteer, part-time, or temporary positions while still maintaining your current employment. This offers both hands-on experience and the chance to extend your professional network to those in this new-to-you specialization. Think of it as a low-risk way to try something on for size. By working hard, even in a volunteer or part-time position, you're also building a professional reputation and expanding your pool of potential references. You might even work yourself right into a new job opportunity.

Informational Interviews

Consider conducting informational interviews with librarians already active in the specialization you're interested in exploring. Informational interviews provide you with an opportunity to sit down with people doing the kind of work you're interested in and to gather information on their career path, expertise, and experience. Informational interviews also provide yet another opportunity to grow your professional network. An informational interview can help you to do several important things:

- Learn from current professionals about the work they do.

- Expand your professional network.

- Explore different types of libraries and positions to clarify your personal career goals.

- Identify your professional strengths and weaknesses as they relate to the positions and libraries you're most interested in.

In preparing for an informational interview, do your research: research the profession, the organization, and the person with whom you will be meeting. You may want to look at general resources that give an overview of the profession. For example, take a look at the U.S. Department of Labor's Occupational Outlook Handbook. You could also look at webpages, annual reports, and statistics for the organization you'll be visiting. Learn more about the person with whom you hope to meet. You want this appointment to be productive, so make sure you're speaking with someone who is active in the field and ready to share his or her story with you. By knowing more about this person (e.g., Is he or she published? Active in professional organizations? In a position you aspire to attain someday?), you'll be better able to shape productive questions for the limited time you have during an informational interview.

Make sure to call, email, or write in advance to ask for an informational appointment, or ask a mutual acquaintance who could refer you. Be sure to be up-front: Tell the person that you have some questions about working in a particular area and would be interested in meeting for an informational interview. Keep the appointment to 20 or 30 minutes. Respect everyone's time, and do not stay longer than originally agreed on unless you are invited to stay longer.

Once you have an appointment scheduled, come prepared with questions and something to take notes with. Remember, this is a two-way conversation. The person you are interviewing may be interested in learning about you in this process, so be prepared to have a conversation and answer questions about yourself.

Before you leave, express your appreciation for the person's time, but never ask for a job. Remember, this is an informational interview only. Do not overstep the limits of the informational interview by asking about employment opportunities or your qualifications for a specific position.

Last, follow up with a written thank-you note within a few days of the interview. Remember, you are not only gaining valuable knowledge about the profession; you're building your professional network. You want to make a good impression.

When you're ready to move from one position, library, or specialization to another, careful planning, preparation, and implementation are crucial for success. Work your professional network to identify opportunities, position yourself to be identified as a competent and trustworthy leader, be creative in your approach, and work diligently toward your professional goals.

8

PUTTING YOURSELF OUT THERE: PRESENTING AND WRITING

Dear Q&A: I keep hearing from colleagues about publishing opportunities and speaking engagements. Is this something I should be doing, too? What will writing and presenting do for my career?

Not everyone wants to put themselves out there. Not everyone wants to present, write, speak in public, or do anything that might mean opening themselves up to possible scrutiny and judgment. Some would rather avoid these projects at all costs, some are content working by themselves in their back offices, and some are extremely intimidated by any form of public communication. Who can blame them? Putting yourself out there can cause anxiety and make your heart race and your palms sweat. We get it. We've been there. We're not saying that everyone needs to put themselves out there in this manner; we are merely suggesting that it doesn't have to be as frightening or as formal as you may think, and that it might be (and most likely *will* be) good for your career, your self-confidence, and your future job prospects.

Writing and presenting are activities that you can do, or may want to do, at any and every stage in your career. Experience and expertise can lead naturally to publishing and presenting but can take some time to acquire. Some people will choose to present and/or write because they want to, others will do it because they need to, and still others will do it simply because the opportunity presents itself. But, no matter what your title is, where you work, or how active (or inactive) you are in the profession, you will—at some point in your career—be asked to speak to, present to, or write for an audience. Even if you do not seek it out, even if you are terrified of public speaking, even if that audience is a small group of colleagues, students, or visitors, you should prepare yourself for this invitation and, just perhaps, start to think about how you might proactively get yourself out there.

What if your job does not require you to write or present? The answer is, You don't need to. Only tenure-track academic librarians might be required to do so, and tenure and promotion requirements will vary considerably by institution. However, you should understand that professional writing and presenting can be done in a variety of ways, and it is quite easy to start small, dip your toes in, and slowly ease your way into the flow. There are many reasons someone might want to write or present, but the main one is that it can boost your career and lead to new and exciting opportunities. If you have any desire to move up the career ladder, move into management positions, take on leadership roles, seek out positions in professional associations, or compete for jobs, writing or presenting can help. And if you do them, even if you don't *have* to, you will be rewarded both personally and professionally: by overcoming a fear, exceeding an expectation, challenging yourself, contributing to the scholarship of the profession, or simply adding to your resume.

The Idea

Whether you are presenting, writing, or both, you always start with an idea. Think about keeping an idea book—a little notepad that you carry around or, for you techies, a tablet, phone, device, or app that allows you to take notes and jot down your ideas. These ideas don't have to be brilliant or unique or mind-blowing; they just have to interest you as ideas you want to pursue. You may have experience or expertise with your idea already, you may start with the desire to gain that expertise, or perhaps the idea *is* the pursuit of experience or expertise. When writing or presenting, your audience needs to feel your interest in or passion for the subject. You don't have to be an expert, and you don't have to be an amazing writer or presenter. You just have to have a good idea, show interest in it, and be able to communicate it to others.

Presenting

If you've ever interviewed, you've presented. If you've led discussions, you've presented. If you've taught a class, you've presented. If you've done a poster session, you've presented. Some presentations may have been planned ahead of time, while others may have been on the fly. We have all spoken in public at some point, whether in classes, in our job, in groups we belong to, or at associations we are involved in. The presentation may not have been formal, and we may not have thought of it as public speaking or presenting, but essentially, any time we talk to a group of people, we are presenting. And the more we do it, the more comfortable we become with it.

You have many different options for getting started with presenting or speaking in public. In your current position, volunteer for committees and be vocal in your contributions, offer to give tours or attend promotional events, and volunteer to teach (or assist with) instruction sessions for your users or your colleagues. Think in terms of professional development for your staff and your colleagues. Do you have a skill that you can teach others? Are you proficient in a specific software, resource, or social media tool? Offer to teach an informal session on it. Teaching is one of the best ways to get started with presenting and speaking, and even though it can be casual and quick, it still requires planning and organization.

Outside your workplace, join associations and special-interest groups and volunteer to coordinate or lead a meeting or event. The more involved you are, the more opportunities there will be. The more you present, the more you will be invited to present. And the more you put yourself out there, the easier it will become. It will develop its own momentum.

The next step is to look for calls for presentations or posters or workshops for local and national organizations, conferences, and symposia. Start small, perhaps with a poster session at a local event or as a moderator for a conference presentation. Small can lead to bigger things. An idea turns into a poster, which can turn into an article, a book chapter, a presentation, or all of the above. Let your ideas grow and become what they want to be, and if they are good ideas, others will notice.

10 Tips for Public Speaking
From Toastmasters International[1]

1. Know your material. *Pick a topic you are interested in. Know more about it than you include in your speech. Use humor, personal stories, and conversational language—that way you won't easily forget what to say.*
2. Practice, practice, practice! *Rehearse out loud with all equipment you plan on using. Revise as necessary.*

Work to control filler words. Practice, pause, and breathe. Practice with a timer and allow time for the unexpected.

3. Know the audience. *Greet some of the audience members as they arrive. It's easier to speak to a group of friends than to strangers.*

4. Know the room. *Arrive early, walk around the speaking area and practice using the microphone and any visual aids.*

5. Relax. *Begin by addressing the audience. It buys you time and calms your nerves. Pause, smile, and count to three before saying anything ("One one-thousand, two one-thousand, three one-thousand. Pause. Begin.). Transform nervous energy into enthusiasm.*

6. Visualize yourself giving your speech. *Imagine yourself speaking, your voice loud, clear, and confident. Visualize the audience clapping—it will boost your confidence.*

7. Realize that people want you to succeed. *Audiences want you to be interesting, stimulating, informative, and entertaining. They're rooting for you.*

8. Don't apologize for any nervousness or problem. *The audience probably never noticed it.*

9. Concentrate on the message—not the medium. *Focus your attention away from your own anxieties and concentrate on your message and your audience.*

10. Gain experience. *Mainly, your speech should represent you—as an authority and as a person. Experience builds confidence, which is the key to effective speaking.*

Writing

If you are a college graduate, you've had to write. If you've written a cover letter, a resume, a letter of intent, or a letter of reference, you've written professionally. You probably write every day in some aspect of your job, whether through an email, a document, a blog post, promotional material, a class description, or something more in-depth. As with presenting, writing for an audience can start small—so small, in fact, that some of what you are already doing may count as professional writing on your resume, such as writing for a blog or a newsletter or writing grant proposals or documentation for resources or systems.

When seeking writing opportunities, look first at local venues. Does your library or an organization that you belong to have a newsletter or a blog you can contribute to? If not, could you start one? Are you involved in a project in your professional career or within your library that might be of interest to others? If so, try writing a brief article about it. Do you have your own professional blog or an idea for one? Do you contribute to professional group discussions online? Do you get to practice your writing?

Remember that writing, like presenting, starts with an idea. You may need to contact some venues, editors, or publishers on your own or answer calls for contributions (for papers, articles, or chapters) with an idea and an abstract. Sometimes you may need to write something first and find a home for it later. We recommend doing all of the above. If you have an idea, start writing. See whether you can complete a brief article (around 1,000 words). Edit it, show it to friends and colleagues, get feedback, and then look for a home for it. If you're lucky, some of the editors you contact may provide constructive feedback. Finally, don't let rejection stop you. We've all been rejected—some of us many times—and it's no fun, but it is part of the publishing process. Just because one publication rejects your article and gives you a poor (or no) reason for doing so doesn't mean the next editor you submit it to won't accept it, with or without revisions. In cases where constructive criticism is offered, rejection can help you improve a given article and even become a better writer.

Use rejection and criticism to push yourself to review, revise, and edit, and then resubmit your work somewhere else.

Before submitting blindly to publications, do your homework. There are probably some publications you read regularly, others you read occasionally, and still others you have never even heard of. Numerous professional journals and blogs, both academic and trade, online and in print, target librarians in various types of libraries doing many different types of work. In other words, there is probably a publication perfectly suited for your writing. If you work in academic libraries and are required to publish (i.e., you are on the tenure track), then you may need to publish in scholarly, peer-reviewed publications, which restricts the type of articles you write. So before you start writing, you should know what is required of you in your current role, what types of publications you need or want to publish in, and what others in your institution are writing or researching. This doesn't mean that you can't write and publish what you want, where you want. You just may need to prioritize your professional writing in order to meet specific requirements or deadlines that are attached to your job. Familiarize yourself with a variety of publications, find ones that appeal to you, and read them regularly to get a sense of the types of articles and types of writing they publish. You can also get good writing ideas just by reading. Every good writer is first a good reader.

Partner Up

Both writing and presenting can be done in partnership with others. This is a good way to start because such things are always less intimidating (and more fun) when you have others to share the burden and the spotlight and to help push you to the finish line. Whether you are with a work buddy or a mentor, part of a panel, or working with someone across the country you've never met, you are still collaborating and feeding off of one another. Take the two of us, for example. We've been co-authoring a column for several years, we've written articles together, and now we are writing a book together. We communicate often, but we've met only a few times in person. We work in very different roles, we belong to different organizations, and we live in different states—and yet it works. Don't limit your partnerships to only those close to you. Seek partnerships online; in professional associations and groups; and in calls for presentations, contributions, and other writing and speaking opportunities. When you find someone you work well with, you may find yourself at the start of a long and rewarding professional collaboration.

GETTING STARTED WITH WRITING AND PRESENTING

A Q&A with Ellen Mehling, job bank manager/career development consultant at the Metropolitan New York Library Council, and director of internships for Long Island University's Palmer School of Library and Information Science

Q: How did you get started presenting?

I started by volunteering for local organizations that serve libraries and librarians. One of the first presentations I did led to an invitation to do another one for pay, and as time went on, I got more invitations to present and to teach classes and workshops. After a while, it developed a momentum of its own: The more presentations I did, the more invitations to do others came my way.

Q: How did you get started writing professionally?

That was also by volunteering for a library-related organization. The presentations I was doing led to professional writing, too, as I was seen as knowledgeable on certain subjects and was asked to write about them. For the first book I contributed to, a colleague forwarded a call for submissions to me, asking if I would be interested in sending something. Opportunities such as that can be found regularly on various email lists.

Q: How have professional writing and presenting shaped your career?

They've led to offers of paid work and additional income, a bigger network, a robust resume, higher visibility online and in the information-professional community, and a way out of a bad situation at a dead-end job in a tough economy. I was fortunate that I realized early in my career that not having any professional writing or public speaking in my work history would put me at a big disadvantage when job hunting.

Both my current jobs were offered to me. There were no applications, resumes, or cover letters to submit, or interviews. The first time I heard of each position was when I was contacted and offered the job. That would not have happened if I hadn't been writing and presenting and getting my name out there.

Q: What are some things information professionals who are interested in writing and presenting should do or not do?

I recommend starting as I did, by offering your services as a volunteer. Library school students can do this while still in school. Get feedback from a trusted friend or someone else in your network as to the quality of your writing and public speaking/ presentations. Whether you are new to the profession or experienced, take care to keep these skills sharp and up-to-date.

If you're interested in working in an academic library, you'll need teaching experience in order to be considered for those types of jobs. Volunteer presentations can be a first step in that direction. Presenting at conferences is another option.

The more experience you can get giving presentations and talks, the better. You'll become more comfortable and confident as time goes by and as you encounter and handle various challenges that can occur during a class or presentation (equipment failure, losing your train of thought, having to shorten or lengthen the presentation on the fly, etc.).

Find your niche—something that interests you and that there is a demand for—and brand yourself. Intentionally shape your online presence and reputation to emphasize the expertise you want to be known for. Stay current on that topic and see if you can connect with others who are already known as authorities on that subject and possibly collaborate with them. Blogging is beneficial, too, for getting your writing out there. You can start a blog yourself or share the writing duties with others.

If you are submitting something for a book or specific journal or website, be sure to read the submission guidelines and follow them exactly. The words you chose so carefully will probably be edited, which can be a bit painful the first couple of times, but that is just part of getting published.

I recommend volunteering throughout your career. I still write and give talks on a volunteer basis, most often on topics related to job hunting and career development. If you have a number of things going on at once, your professional identity won't be tied to one job or one employer.

Don't focus on getting paid for your writing and presenting, especially in the beginning. Do it without anticipation of reward. You are proving yourself and building a reputation and trust among other professionals; this takes time. If you do it with expectations, you will enjoy it less, and it may have the opposite of the desired effect on your career because people will learn to question your motives. Do it to serve your network and the profession, and trust that in the long run, the career benefits will come your way.

The Art of Speaking and Writing Well

Every professional should be able to speak and write well. These are skills that need to be honed and practiced, and they will come more naturally for some than for others. Our profession depends on sharing, communicating, and learning from others. We need our librarians to write, present, and speak about what they've done and how they've done it and to offer ideas, suggestions, and research that will inform the rest of us and lead us all into the future. Some library professionals, after putting themselves out there over and over again, have realized that 1) they *are* good at it and 2) they can even make a career out of it.

Even if you are not required or encouraged to present or write for your job, doing so will only enhance your resume and your career. Speaking and writing are essential skills for supervisors, managers, and leaders, as well as for those who are seeking jobs or promotions. If we think of them as communication skills, which they are, then we would say "of course" we need to have those skills. Of course, we need to be able to communicate with our colleagues, the public, students, faculty, and our specific clientele. Of course, we need to be able to instruct our users, train our staff, document our procedures, and evaluate ourselves. Of course, we need to be able to write and speak well. Of course.

Endnote

1. "10 Tips for Public Speaking," *Toastmasters International*, accessed July 10, 2013, www.toastmasters.org/tips.asp.

$$Q\&A$$

9

JOB FLEXIBILITY:
POSSIBILITY OR MYTH?

Dear Q&A: There are a lot of things I like about my job, but the one thing that seems to be missing is some kind of flexibility. I mean, I am more than my job, right? Do flexible positions exist, and if so, how do I find one?

Doesn't everyone crave flexibility? Doesn't everyone want more control of when and where they work? Life is not just about jobs or the 5-day workweek. We are not just employees, not just librarians, and not just nine-to-fivers. We are mothers and fathers, sons and daughters, siblings and friends. We are renters and land owners. We are commuters. We are students, teachers, and entrepreneurs. We are writers and presenters, thinkers and doers. Yet there are times when these other aspects of our lives disrupt our careers and work schedules, and we are forced to make decisions that may affect not just our current job but future jobs as well. Flexibility and an employer who supports our needs outside work can mean the difference between staying in a job and leaving for something else—or just leaving.

Flexibility in the workplace can mean various things: an informal or formal arrangement, which can be temporary, short-term, long-term, or permanent. It might be called an alternative work schedule, flextime, or variable work schedule. Some jobs or roles were created to be flexible, while others morph into flexible ones. However you describe it, and for whatever reason you need it, flexibility in the workplace will continue to be a necessity for many employees. If we value the growth of our profession, we need to incorporate a certain amount of flexibility into everyone's schedule and into every work environment.

Libraries themselves need to be flexible in order to accommodate their users. All libraries are in a constant state of flux as budgets shrink, prices rise, technology advances, and resources and services move to different formats. It makes sense, especially in times of adversity and change, that library employees be allowed more control over their schedules in order to maintain morale, encourage productivity, and promote a willingness to do more with less.

Flexibility in Libraries

In an article on how workplace inflexibility may be affecting libraries, Michael Germano makes the following observation: "Cutbacks, layoffs and furloughs have demanded that libraries reduce operating hours and services as well as materials. By choosing to embrace flexibility in terms of hours and location, managers can indeed mitigate the impact of these cuts by producing more engaged, happier employees who are willing to work different hours delivering services through alternate means that depend little upon the old-fashioned constraints of a traditional library work environment."[1]

Some companies or institutions are inherently more liberal than others when it comes to flexible work schedules. Some jobs come with built-in flextime for research, writing, presenting, or traveling. Some librarians are eligible to take semester-long or even year-long sabbaticals. New mothers in many larger U.S. organizations are by law given leave time (sometimes with pay) under the Family and Medical Leave Act if certain requirements are met. As well, employees can take short-term leave to care for an ill family member or recover from an illness or accident. For these types of temporary arrangements that are already built into the system, you should speak with your supervisor or human resources department.

Some jobs are more flexible than others. Certain types of roles and specific sets of skills lend themselves more naturally to working remotely (telecommuting) or working flexible hours. The obvious roles are ones that involve more technology and less public service. So if you deal with electronic resource management, systems, web design, instructional design, or distance learning, much of your job is already online, and you may have a good chance of converting your position into a more flexible one. Other roles can be done partially online or remotely, such as jobs in cataloging and access services or interlibrary loan. In these types of positions, librarians can potentially use a virtual private network to access their work computers in order to use the proprietary software or systems needed for their jobs. In other types of roles that are more people- or materials-oriented, such as reference, instruction, circulation, reserves, and serials and collection management and administration, working remotely may not be your best flexible option.

If you think you may need to have more flexible hours than your position provides, or if you will need at some point to reduce your hours or have a different and more permanent type of flexible schedule, it is time to start planning now.

CAREER TRANSITIONS AND FLEXIBILITY

Priscilla K. Shontz, editor for LIScareer.com

When I reflect on my career path so far, one theme stands out: flexibility. My career path has curved, swerved, and branched out in unexpected directions because of life changes and personal growth. This isn't uncommon, of course. No one knows what he or she will be doing—or will *want* to be doing—20 or 30 years after graduation. Diversifying your education and experience can set you up to adapt to the inevitable changes that you'll face.

My undergraduate student job in a library led me into the field of librarianship. As an LIS student, I was most interested in working in academic libraries because of my experience and because, like many students, I enjoyed being on a college campus. When I graduated, unemployment was high. I sent out more than 100 resumes (nationwide) and got three interviews. Having previous library experience and being willing to relocate were very helpful in my first job search.

My first job was in a five-person community college library in a small rural town. Working in a small library proved to be an outstanding learning experience because I was able to participate in a wide variety of tasks. That diverse experience helped enable me to move into a supervisory position at a private university in a large city. In that tenure-track position, I was prompted to start writing articles, attend conferences, and become active in professional associations. A supervisor there encouraged me to pursue my interest in career topics. That job launched me into networking and publishing.

During that time, I met and married my husband. We moved to a coastal city, where he returned to school. I worked in a two-person medical library in a hospital that had contracted its library services to the local university. This position gave me a chance to work in a special library, do medical research, and learn skills such as serials management while working at both the hospital and the university libraries.

When my husband graduated, his new job took us to a major urban area. I began working as a branch manager of a public library. I met many inspiring colleagues and learned more about the huge community service role that public libraries play. I then started writing my first book and began working part-time serving distance education students in multiple campuses of a university system.

When we began our family, I decided to stay home, at least while our children were young. I continued writing library career books as a way to stay active in the profession and maintain connections with colleagues. I also launched LIScareer.com and began soliciting, editing, and publishing articles on that site.

While my children were in preschool, I worked as the librarian at their private school. It was adding elementary-level classes, so I set up a new library and provided library and computer lab services. This experience taught me that, like teachers, school librarians need strong classroom management skills and spend a lot of time outside work preparing lessons and resources.

I've continued to write and to publish articles on LIScareer.com for more than 12 years now. For a few years, I also offered online career consulting services through LIScareer.com. I met some fascinating people but did not feel the return on investment was high enough to continue the service, at least at that time. Freelance writing offers me the flexibility to be available to help my family and my aging parents and to volunteer extensively at my children's schools. It also keeps me connected and active in the library community. I don't know where my career path will lead, but I hope to be prepared for opportunities and open to change.

What advice might I give based on my own experiences? Stay flexible. Try not to get pigeonholed. Be open to unexpected opportunities. Every job, course, volunteer experience, and so on adds to your repertoire of skills and contacts. If you diversify your experience, you could be better prepared to shift in different directions in the future.

Types of Flexible Work

Flexible work falls into many categories:

- *Compressed work week:* In this case, an employee works longer hours per day and fewer days (e.g., four 10-hour days rather than five 8-hour days).

- *Part-time:* This is any case in which an employee works less than the regular full-time work week.

- *Flextime:* This arrangement allows an employee to have a more flexible workday (e.g., come in earlier and leave earlier; come in later and leave later; or work different hours on different days).

- *Telecommuting:* Essentially, this means working remotely, most commonly at home. This type of work arrangement is not possible for some people and is largely dependent on the type of work the employee does.

- *Job sharing:* This arrangement allows for two or more people to share a particular job. Typically, they would work on different days and different hours to cover all aspects of the job.

Pursuing a Flexible Schedule in Your Current Workplace

There are several steps you should take once you decide you want
or need a more flexible schedule:

1. *Gather information.* Talk to your supervisor or director,
   human resources, your union (if you have one), and others
   in your library or your institution who have flexible
   schedules. Ask questions. Get feedback from others who
   have more longevity than you do. But even if no one in
   your organization has tried a flexible schedule, you can
   still be successful.

2. *Think about the culture of your library or organization.* Is
   it open to flexibility and change? Is it supportive of its
   employees? Are the managers easy to talk to? Does it
   encourage communication and professional development?

3. *Track your work.* Keep a log of everything you do, and
   where and how you do it.

4. *Figure out what your ideal schedule would be.* Do you
   want or need to reduce your hours? Do you need to work
   different hours? Is this temporary or permanent? When do
   you want or need this new schedule to begin?

5. *Figure out how your role and your duties will be covered.*
   How will your new schedule impact your co-workers, the
   library, and its services? This is especially important if you
   need to reduce your hours. How will things get done? Is
   there someone else in your library who can help complete
   your work? Are you able to do your work from home or
   another location? How will you track your work and your
   hours?

6. *Write up a proposal.* Include the information, evidence,
   ideas, and solutions you have compiled.

7. *Figure out what you will do if your proposal is not
   accepted.* Will you resign? Will you ask for a leave of

absence? Will you continue to work your regular schedule? You should imagine different scenarios and be prepared to follow through on your decisions.

8. *Meet with your supervisor.* Present your proposal, and prepare to negotiate.

For some people, working as a librarian or in a library role just isn't feasible, because the position just can't provide the flexibility they need. We all have priorities in our lives. For many of us, our careers take a backseat to our families or our health at some point. If that means we need to leave a job, take a different type of job, or wait until we can find a job that provides us with the flexibility, security, and innovation that we crave, then we need to adapt, adjust, and figure out how to move forward in our careers during those times when we seem to be standing still.

THOUGHTS ON FLEXIBLE WORK ARRANGEMENTS

Laura Schimming, information and education services librarian at the Mount Sinai School of Medicine, New York, NY

In my library career, I have had the opportunity to work full-time, part-time, a combination of part-time and telecommuting, and 100 percent telecommuting. Having a library administration that has worked with me to develop flexible working plans and opportunities has definitely given me a better work–life balance, for which I am grateful.

I first approached my library director to ask for part-time hours while expecting the birth of twins. I knew that I wanted to continue my career but that I was also really going to need some flexibility while caring for newborn twins. Fortunately, my library director agreed to a trial part-time work arrangement. I don't really know why she decided to say yes initially, but I would like to think it was partly because she valued the contributions I had made during my previous 6 years of employment at the library. After a 6-month trial period, my director, immediate supervisor, and I all agreed that the part-time arrangement was working, and it became permanent.

A year later, a staff reorganization and hiring freeze created more work than library staff could handle. I was offered the chance to work from home 1 day per week, in addition to keeping my in-office hours. At this point, I began to take on more eresource management responsibilities that fit well with telecommuting. A few years and another baby later, my husband took a job in another state, and my administration approached me about continuing my part-time work strictly as a telecommuter.

These flexible work arrangements have definitely had a positive impact on my family. Contributing to a career that I enjoy while also having weekday time with my children has made me both a better mother and a better employee. I have been able to save (at least a little bit) on child care expenses by enrolling my children in part-time rather than full-time care and, when projects are flexible enough, by working at night after the kids are asleep.

Working part-time is a bit different from telecommuting, and both provide some challenges. Although I work only part-time, I often feel as if I have full-time responsibilities. I find myself checking and responding to email on my days off so as not to delay a group project, stall the resolution of a library access problem, or slow down another shared task. I sometimes have to remind myself that I am not being paid for extra hours. The main challenge with telecommuting exclusively is not interacting in person with both colleagues and library users. We use Skype, email, and phone calls to *stay in touch, but of course I miss out on the daily social interactions and impromptu problem solving that take place in person.*

On the whole, I find that the negatives of flexible work arrangements are far outweighed by the positives. Working part-time and from home is rewarding, fits well with digital library work, and potentially offers a good work–life balance. I hope that more employers will consider offering flexible options to their librarians.

Finding a Flexible Job

Whether you're leaving a current job to find one with more flexibility or whether you're re-entering the workforce hoping to find a flexible position, searching for a job is a difficult process. Knowing that you need to find one that can offer flexibility is downright tricky. Here are some tips for hunting and interviewing for flexible jobs:

- Use job search tools specific to flexible or part-time jobs, such as FlexJobs (www.flexjobs.com).

- Look for keywords in the job description, such as *flexible hours*, *evenings or weekends*, *alternative schedule*, or *virtual services*.

- Look for jobs dependent on technology, ones that (potentially) you could do remotely.

- Research the library or institution and find out what kinds of services they offer at different times of the day.

- If you are looking for part-time work, seek *only* part-time or hourly jobs.

- Don't mention flexibility in your cover letter unless it is stated explicitly in the job description.

- When interviewing, ask about possible flextime or alternative work schedules, but don't state that you have to have flexibility. Now is not the time to make demands.

- The right time to mention the type of schedule you prefer (or need) and why is when you get a job offer. Don't expect to hear "yes" immediately or at all. But if the organization wants to hire you, it may be able to work flexibility into your schedule.

 ## *And the Survey Says ...*

We received a variety of responses when we asked the question, What arrangements did you make with your employer to adjust your professional responsibilities to accommodate major life events?

- *I now work a compressed work week (Monday through Thursday) and am still considered full time. Having the extra weekday off has been of tremendous value to my family.*

- *With hip replacement, then a broken femur, and then knee replacement, I trained our receptionist to help students in the library. I communicated with staff and students via phone and email and continued my online teaching from home.*

- *I arranged to work a modified work schedule 3 days a week.*

- *I took time off, but there is someone on staff who also has my skills. We are backups for each other.*

- *Most of my professional responsibilities were transferred to a well-qualified temporary library director. What could not be transferred, I completed while on maternity leave.*

- *I flexed my hours, worked from home, and worked with students through social media.*

- *It is complicated, but our human resources (HR) department was able to allow me to buy additional leave with my state disability money. Staff donated sick leave hours to my account. I was on a liberal work schedule—working either remotely or in-house when I could.*
- *The two major accommodations that have allowed me to advance professionally in spite of family responsibilities are telecommuting and flexible scheduling.*
- *I worked overtime when I could, communicated and shared work with others, and helped others when they were on leave. You have to know your rights and be sure to communicate your rights to the employer when you ask for leave.*
- *I delegated my work to others for the bulk of my time off. It was good for all of us as everyone developed new skills as a result.*
- *The reality was that telecommuting is a taboo topic here, and ultimately my supervisor wasn't comfortable negotiating with HR for this kind of accommodation. I do have a lot of flexibility with when I come in and when I leave, so at least if I'm a little late or leave a little early, there isn't any pushback. It's understood that I also work "informally" from home often and that it's a professional position (i.e., not a clock-punching, time-sensitive position).*
- *I used all my vacation and sick time. But management did not make it easy and threatened to not allow me to do it more than once.*
- *I could not make any arrangements for accommodation. I had to quit.*
- *I went from tenure track full-time to part-time term.*
- *There weren't any accommodations. I was laid off.*

- *My manager knew what was going on in my personal life. I talked with the HR department, and we developed a plan together. I was able to take leave when I needed it because we had planned this in advance. I was also able to bank hours and take them off when I needed to. My work hours were flexible, which also helped.*

Endnote

1. Michael A. Germano, "Does Workplace Inflexibility Cost Libraries?" *Library Worklife: HR E-News for Today's Leaders*, March 2010, accessed July 10, 2013, ala-apa.org/newsletter/2010/03/28/does-workplace-inflexibility-cost-libraries.

10

Alternative Jobs: The Nontraditional Career Path

Dear Q&A: If I wanted to use my MLS outside libraries, do you have any recommendations about where I should look? Are there other places and industries that value the skills I've honed in my library work?

The word *librarian* implies someone who works in a library or someone who works with books. If you tell someone you are a librarian, they ask you what library, and then they tell you how lucky you must be to read books all day. Because that is what we do, right? Because *library* is right in our title, it defines our role, our career, and our profession. But in today's technology-focused, information-laden workplaces, is it more accurate to call us information professionals? Do we need the library (literally or symbolically) to define what we do? Do we need to work in a building full of books to be librarians?

In the *Atlas of New Librarianship*, R. David Lankes writes, "I have long contended that a room full of books is simply a closet but that an empty room with a librarian in it is a library."[1] Perhaps we have been classifying ourselves too rigidly, and we should allow our roles, our degrees, our titles, and our profession a little room to expand, grow, and diversify. After all, many of us have graduated with *information* degrees, and many of us have already assimilated seamlessly into roles in other industries.

We know that librarians are good at finding information, researching and synthesizing data, organizing and classifying materials, maintaining and preserving items, providing access to resources, and educating others about how to use systems and tools. We should also know that we don't need to work in libraries to be information professionals, and we don't need to be called a *librarian* to do the work of one. It's no surprise that library (or information) skills are used, sought after, and valued in other professions and that the skills we learn in graduate school and while working in libraries can help us obtain nontraditional professional positions both within and outside libraries. We have many opportunities beyond a traditional, typical librarian job in a traditional, typical library.

The Information Field

The iSchools organization addresses the changing information profession: "The information field is the rapidly evolving profession of our time. Just as business careers and MBAs became de rigueur in the industrial age, information professionals are now in high demand, as businesses and society grapple with the challenges and opportunities of the digital age."[2]

The skills we are known for—finding, evaluating, synthesizing, classifying, and providing access to information—are all skills that are useful, and even desired, in many different professions—earning them their reputation as "transferable skills." They can include skills in customer service, technology, writing, management, communications, research, teaching, languages, and marketing, to name just a few. Transferable skills can help you get jobs in libraries when you have little or no library experience, and they can help you get jobs outside libraries.

In *Library Journal*'s 2011 placement survey for library school graduates, 18.3 percent of placements were in sectors outside library and information science (LIS). These graduates found jobs in a variety of roles in nonprofit agencies (17.3 percent), private industry (30 percent), and other areas, including law, finance, and retail (52.7 percent). "Finding employment outside of the LIS professions became a delicate balancing act for many. Besides jobs in nonprofits and private industry, the graduating class also found employment in an array of 'other' agencies but often using the skills learned during their master's degree programs." Some of these jobs fell into the following areas: software engineering, user interface design, digital asset management, analytics, grant writing, fundraising, government, biotech firms, advertising, marketing, television, higher education, hospitals, and publishing.[3]

Exploring Options

G. Kim Dority, author of Rethinking Information Work *and* LIS Career Sourcebook, *illuminates the challenge of choosing a career direction in library science:*

> *There are so many directions to take your library science career that part of the challenge is figuring out which of those directions to pursue first. However, sometimes it helps to frame the*

choices as categories of options. From librarian to independent information professional, these may include:

- Traditional library jobs: *Working within facilities-based librarianship, such as becoming a school librarian, public librarian, or campus-based academic librarian (although it's increasingly the case that few types of librarianship can any longer be thought of as "traditional")*

- Merging nontraditional with traditional: *Doing nontraditional things within a traditional library setting (perhaps creating unique outreach programs for the local small-business community)*

- Librarian with a twist: *Performing traditional library roles but within an organization whose mission is not librarianship or education (the traditional special library role)*

- Going special within special: *Doing nontraditional types of librarian work within traditional special libraries (e.g., designing and running the company intranet)*

- Becoming part of the ops team: *Doing these nontraditional activities embedded in operational units rather than in a designated organization library (for example, being the researcher on a business-development team)*

- Supporting the cause: *Doing library-focused activities outside of but for libraries and librarians (think vendors, bibliographic utilities, etc.)*

- Bridging: *Building on skills honed in a library-based job to bridge those skills into a new, nonlibrary role (for example, shifting your reference librarian skills to competitive intelligence or prospect research)*
- Making it up: *Creating your own job, either within a library or for a nonlibrary organization*
- Going solo: *Going independent, or doing any of the activities that fall within these categories on a freelance, contract, or project basis—an increasingly popular information professional path*[4]

The definition of "alternative jobs for librarians" is broad and varied and can encompass a variety of different roles, settings, and industries. An alternative career might involve a traditional librarian job in a nontraditional setting, working in a nontraditional role within a library setting, or something else entirely. The types of industries that hire and use the skills of information professionals are too many to name—and in reality, they could be any industry in any setting. As library schools continue to graduate more and more information professionals, and as librarians nearing or at retirement age continue to work longer and longer in their jobs, those who are searching for jobs may need to look outside libraries and outside traditional roles in order to find employment. That's OK, and even kind of exciting. We think that a good motto to live by when job seeking is "Keep an open mind, and cast a wide net."

You may already know that you want to do something different or something out of the ordinary. Maybe you have a dream of starting your own business; pursuing more education; or becoming a teacher, writer, consultant, or designer. Maybe you find yourself unsatisfied, unsupported, or unengaged in your current position and feel an urge to move on to something else. Perhaps it was always your plan to use your degree in a nontraditional setting or role. Maybe something (a job offer, a concept, or a desire to try something different) serendipitously fell into your lap. Perhaps you've been looking for a job for a while and have been unable to secure a librarian position within a library. Whatever scenario describes your situation, it is always a good idea to keep an open mind when it comes to jobs. Know what you are good at and what you really enjoy doing, which means that you will need to assess your skills and goals, seek different places to search for jobs, and be able to revise and rework your application materials for different types of industries.

Assessing Strengths

In What's the Alternative? Career Options for Librarians and Info Pros, *Rachel Singer Gordon provides wise advice for assessing your job strengths:*

> *Once you have a general picture of what you want in your career, think about the skills, talents, and knowledge you already possess that can help you get to that point. Finding new ways to use and develop the skills you have acquired as an information professional (as well as those you've picked up through previous careers, education, or interests) is essential from the moment you begin to contemplate an alternative path. Skills and strengths that may be tangential or even unused in your current job may*

grow to become integral to your new career; those that you think of only in the library context can be reframed and used in other contexts. This can sometimes be as simple as changing the language you use to describe what you do.[5]

How to Get Started

Before you make the move toward an alternative career, take some time to examine, or re-examine, your goals, assess your skills and your strengths, and categorize your assets. Your skills, strengths, and assets include any that will support you in your career move, as well as your personal interests (things you love doing), which will add to your motivation. Also evaluate your weaknesses; they help you determine the skills, experience, knowledge, and contacts you need to acquire.

Talk to some people who have successfully made the move into alternative positions or nontraditional industries and ventured into unknown waters. Gain as much insight and information as you can about the particular professions and industries that interest you, and start thinking about how you can market yourself to them.

As always, you should revise and change your materials for every single job application. Each job is unique. As always, you need to make it clear to potential employers that you want *their* job, not just a job. When applying for jobs outside libraries, seek examples of resumes for specific industries and roles. Carefully read their requirements for application materials, which may be completely different from those you are accustomed to and those prescribed for librarian positions. You may be used to writing two-page cover letters and sending in a three- to four-page resume or curriculum vitae. These specifications may not work for jobs outside libraries. You may need to condense and include only highly relevant information. You may want to look at different ways of formatting your resume. Consider a functional resume (discussed in Chapter 3), which works well with transferable skills and allows you to put your most relevant experience and skills up front.

 ## *And the Survey Says ...*

Susan L., a research analyst, notes:

> *I was able to transition successfully from a research librarian to a researcher (outside libraries) and then to an analyst, which I am today, because of four things: 1) Maintaining strong relationships with professionals ... so strong that over the years, those professionals have become good friends. 2) Continually building research and database skills. That means building a reputation that you're the first to know emerging trends, solutions, and tools. People will come to you. 3) Whether at work or play, be helpful where you can add value. That means offering an opinion or advice when asked (when people are ready to hear) and making sure you don't spread yourself too thin by being helpful to every single person in your company. 4) Manage your time. Make sure you have enough juice to last the week. Burning out helps no one. Rather it's detrimental to your health and can cast a shadow on your ability to perform.*

Finding an Alternative Job

Even if *librarian* is part of the job title or if the position is located in a library, certain jobs may not be listed in the usual librarian job-seeking sites, publications, or email lists. You will need to broaden your search and seek more job ads. Use the mega job sites such as Monster.com, SimplyHired.com, and CareerBuilder.com. These sites categorize their job listings into broad areas or industries such as information technology, research, government, marketing, healthcare, publishing, customer service, and education, which you can use to help you narrow your search. You should also look at online newspaper ads, trade publications and websites, and association sites that list job ads in other industries. If you don't know where a certain industry may be posting its jobs, contact a human resources department at a specific company and ask. Certain companies may post in only a few places, so be relentless in your search.

When searching for alternative jobs, you may need to think outside the box and outside the librarian mind-set. Other companies or industries may use unfamiliar terminology in their job titles and descriptions. Try searching with skill-based keywords and ones that you may already have listed on your resume. Here are examples:

- Assessment
- Classification
- Content management
- Design
- Development
- Instruction
- Marketing
- Metadata
- Outreach
- Project development
- Research
- Systems
- Taxonomy
- Training

- User experience
- Writing

LEAVING A 20-YEAR CAREER TO PURSUE A STARTUP BUSINESS

Pam Sessoms, LibraryH3lp

Vendor. I've struggled with that word. Vendors are the people you can't trust, the ones who are only out for your library's money. Right?

I am here to tell you that it's not always like that. My husband, Eric, is a brilliant programmer, and he (quite unexpectedly) sat up and declared that he'd help me solve a particularly nasty technical problem involving chat and IM reference services back in 2008. This particular problem wasn't really practical to solve within an actual library at the time: too few programmers with the chops and time to focus on the problem; too much political risk; too few ways to handle the inevitable sustainability questions (i.e., how are we going to pay for the care and feeding of this beast?).

So away we went, building and growing a thing called LibraryH3lp (libraryh3lp.com). From 2008 to 2011, he coded while I tested, did troubleshooting, documented, and offered user support on the side, at the same time keeping a full-time librarian job. LibraryH3lp made a lot of librarians and patrons pretty happy, with more than 300 libraries using the product. What about the sustainability question? Our effort was a mostly accidental startup just seeking to solve a technical problem, so Eric didn't have a grant or investors or anything like that. He decided to charge a minimal but fair fee in exchange for a good product. *Scandalous!* Who does that these days?! And he built LibraryH3lp from the ground up for openness and good interoperability with other systems.

By the end of 2011, I was pretty tired—honestly, I was approaching a nervous breakdown. I loved my "real librarian" job. I worked with brilliant colleagues amid a sea of incredible resources. But I also loved working on LibraryH3lp. Having raised that puppy from birth and having used it extensively in real practice, I was pretty much uniquely qualified to work on it and shape its continued development.

In the end, I made the difficult decision to leave my "real job" and pursue LibraryH3lp full-time. So here I am. As of this writing, I've been away from the university for about 6 months. I miss my colleagues and all that goes with working as part of a team in one of the best research libraries in the world. But I also love working from home and listening to my dog snore. I don't miss the daily commute. I don't miss the paperwork. I really adore having to rely on my alarm clock much less. Now that I'm doing LibraryH3lp full-time, I handle a lot of day-to-day business things, such as billing and invoicing. Surprisingly, I enjoy that sort of thing, for now, anyway. It's methodical, almost meditative, in its routine.

Then there is the measure of unpredictability. Just a couple of weeks ago, the library reference world was rocked by the announcement that Google had acquired Meebo, used by many libraries for chat reference services, and would be shutting down nearly all of Meebo's services in 1 month. I think I've worked about 16 hours a day since that announcement. At least two other, much larger companies have announced new chat reference products, and this has been one of my first tastes of real private-market competition. But I guess that is life as a vendor, and it is true that competition creates better products.

Some of the challenges that libraries face are difficult to solve from inside the library for logistical and financial reasons, and these may be better tackled from the private sphere of the library ecosystem. But libraries have created some amazing services and infrastructure by building on their cooperative spirit and very strong political and technical ties to each other. The very notion of interlibrary loan still simply thrills me, as do the ideas behind things such as single copy and large scale digitization.

In summary, I love my new work and the flexibility of self-employment. Granted, it is not as stable and secure, but I love change and learning new things all the time. I have not been in my new role for long enough to really begin to understand the interplay between open technical systems, the free market, and existing library systems. But moving ahead, I hope tiny little inroads can be made so that library companies can become a bit more like the libraries we serve.

Selling My Degree to People Outside Libraries

When looking for jobs outside the library profession, for alternative roles within libraries, or for roles that do not require an MLS (or equivalent), you might need to do more prep work, change your game plan, and display a little extra savvy. You may need to convince potential employers that your skills, experience, and degree are right for the job, whatever that job may be. You may need to answer questions about why you don't want to work in libraries or at least in a traditional librarian position. You may need to change people's perceptions of librarianship and the information profession. You may need to talk about how your degree is exactly what is needed for the job at hand. When interviewing, the most important things to remember are to be approachable and professional, express enthusiasm, ask questions, and show confidence. You need to believe that you can successfully use your skills, experience, and degree in nontraditional, alternative positions.

And the Survey Says ...

We asked, If you were to look for a position in which you could use your skills and your MLS degree outside a library, what would it be (or what area would it be in)*? Here are the most popular responses we received:*

- Archivist
- Bookstore owner
- Career counselor
- College recruiter
- Communications
- Competitive intelligence
- Computer applications
- Concierge
- Consultant
- Corporate marketing researcher
- Data management/analysis
- Ecommerce
- Editor
- Education/educational technology
- Entrepreneur
- Event planning
- Fact checker
- Financial management
- Fundraising
- GIS/informatics
- Grant writing
- Historic preservation
- Human resources
- Independent info broker
- Indexing
- Interface design
- Knowledge manager
- Library interior design
- Marketing
- Medical research
- Paralegal
- Policy research
- Product development
- Public relations
- Publishing
- Real estate broker
- Records management
- Reporter
- Researcher
- Social work
- Taxonomist
- Think tank
- Trainer
- Video production
- Web content management
- Website designer
- Writer

Going Back to Libraries

After some time in an alternative career or work outside libraries (by choice or by necessity), you may think about moving back into a more traditional position. Don't assume that your work outside libraries means that you don't have the skills, experience, and motivation that library employers are looking for. In fact, your unique skills, honed outside the LIS sector, might just be the tipping factor that lands you a job in a library. Let's face it, diversification is a growing trend, and the right experience (no matter where it was acquired) is a precious commodity. In any organization, people want to hire the best candidate, the one who most closely matches the needs of the position and the organization. It will be your job as that candidate to educate those making the hiring decision and to show that your skills, although gained in a different environment, will transfer to their organization and make you the best qualified candidate. So take the time to assess your skills and then translate them into the language of the job you want. Revise your application materials and be prepared to discuss how your skills and your experience closely match the needs of the organization. Most important, believe that you can transition out of, and back into, libraries because your skills and your education are valued.

TAKING THE ALTERNATIVE PATH

Carrie Netzer Wajda, new business librarian at Y&R, New York, NY

In library school, there can be a lot of pressure to choose a particular track (academic vs. corporate vs. public libraries) before you even gain any real-world experience working in libraries. I graduated from my MLIS program with 8 years of paraprofessional experience and an iron determination to find a research-oriented tenure-track librarian position. I immediately plunged into a subject master's degree program and pursued every academic opportunity that might lead to the kind of role I coveted.

Yet just 5 months after the ink had dried on my second master's diploma, I quit my academic librarian job to start a freelance writing and research business. After 5 years of postgraduate, professional-level academic library experience, that tenure-track research role seemed as remote a career possibility as ever. I was burned out from teaching too many classes, long commutes to distant jobs, bureaucracy, and low pay. I figured it couldn't be that hard to earn something close to my library salary with freelance work, and if I wasn't going to make a lot of money, I might as well focus on the kind of work I enjoyed: research and writing.

And it worked! Although no one at library school ever mentioned such a possibility, there is plenty of freelance work out there for librarians. While running a business isn't easy, it's no harder than dragging oneself to a disappointing job every day. But you have to treat it like a business to be successful, which means doing many things they don't teach in library school: marketing of your skills, project management, and client management.

The arrival of my first child made my burgeoning freelance career extremely challenging to manage, so when a part-time permanent role with an advertising firm became available, I applied. While I had never worked in advertising or any other kind of corporate library, I had written for marketers, and my teaching experience was a natural fit for the global training sessions I now conduct. But the most important reason I got the job was my ability to apply my skills in different contexts. Focus on developing skill sets—especially technical skills and the "soft" skills of people management—and you'll find that those purported barriers between librarian career paths largely disappear.

Here are my tips for transitioning between careers:

- Employers worth working for hire *skills* as much as they do *direct job experience.* If a potential employer is too hidebound to consider your skills just because you acquired them in a different context, that employer is probably going to be inflexible in other ways as well. (You still have to make the case that your skills really are transferable, of course.)

- A well-written job description helps you identify what an employer is looking for. If you can't tell from the job description, then the employer may not really know what he or she wants in a candidate.
- A great resume and cover letter are essential for getting your foot in the door, but at the interview, it's all about you. No matter how good you are on paper, it's what you do and how you present yourself in the interview that will determine whether you get the job.
- Look for part-time, freelance, or even unpaid opportunities that will help you develop and expand your skills. Even small projects can have a big impact on your career, but select your projects wisely for maximum impact on your marketability.
- Don't limit your career options prematurely. Think about what you enjoy doing on a day-to-day basis, and look for career opportunities that match your interests, wherever you may find them.
- Be patient and flexible. Most people don't have linear careers, and careers develop over decades. What's right for you can change with time, and that's OK.

Endnotes

1. R. David Lankes, *The Atlas of New Librarianship* (Boston: MIT Press, 2011), 16.
2. "The Information Field," *iSchools*, accessed July 10, 2013, ischools.org/about/the-information-field.
3. Stephanie L. Maatta, "Placements & Salaries 2012: Types of Placements," *Library Journal,* October 15, 2012, accessed July 10, 2013, lj.libraryjournal.com/2012/10/placements-and-salaries/2012-survey/types-of-placements.

4. G. Kim Dority, *Rethinking Information Work: A Career Guide for Librarians and Other Information Professionals* (Westport, CT: Libraries Unlimited, 2006).

5. Rachel Singer Gordon, *What's the Alternative? Career Options for Librarians and Info Pros* (Medford, NJ: Information Today, Inc., 2008), 12.

Part Three
Finishing Stages

"Why, except as a means of livelihood, a man should desire to act on the stage when he has the whole world to act in, is not clear to me."

—George Bernard Shaw

11

Moving Up the Ladder: Stepping Into Management

> *Dear Q&A: I'm looking for a new challenge. I'm profes-*
> *sionally active and have chaired a lot of library commit-*
> *tees, but I don't supervise anyone, and I'm not in*
> *management. How do I build new advancement opportu-*
> *nities into my work without scaring my supervisor and*
> *making him think I want to leave (or worse, that I want*
> *his job!)?*

When looking for new challenges and ways to move forward in your career, you've got to have a plan. Whether your goals are short-term, long-term, or somewhere in the middle, it's important to have a career plan that allows you to set reasonable career goals that will help you shape a successful and satisfying career.

Developing a Plan

When thinking about your career in the short- and long-term, consider what you like most about your current situation and what seems to be missing. Create a list of SMART[1] goals, and break each goal into actionable steps. While the SMART concept originated as a way for management to set performance objectives, it's also a solid approach to creating personal and professional goals at the individual level. The words associated with each letter have evolved during the years and can vary by situation; when creating your career plan, aim for goals that are:

- Specific: Are goals precise, detailed, clear, and not too general?

- Measurable: How do you define achievement and success?

- Attainable: Is this something you can achieve?

- Relevant: Does it matter? If it matters, it's worth the effort.

- Time bound: What's the due date? Setting a deadline drives commitment and urgency.

For example, if you want to be a supervisor but lack supervisory experience, set professional goals to gain it:

- Specific: Gain introductory supervisory experience.

- Measurable: Have at least one direct report (temp, student, or permanent employee).

- Attainable: Develop a new project, with the opportunity to hire new employees.

- Relevant: Make sure the project is important and coincides with interest in supervision, since supervisory experience is necessary to advance a career.

- Timely: Within 6 months of the project's start, evaluate quality of supervisory experience gained.

Look for opportunities to supervise student assistants, volunteers, or temporary employees, working your way into supervising permanent employees. Another way to gain supervisory experience is by taking the lead on a significant project. Although this doesn't give you direct supervisory experience, you will gain valuable related skills (e.g., directing, delegating, and evaluating work) that will transfer nicely into future supervisory positions. Whatever your goals, develop a plan that identifies each step and its desired outcome, relevance, and time frame.

Another way to develop a career plan is to talk with a mentor. If you're lucky enough to have a mentor already, your career path and plans should be an ongoing part of your conversations. If you haven't yet found a mentor, now's the time. Investigate mentor opportunities through your place of employment, your alumni association, or your professional association. You may also identify colleagues in your professional community who have similar career interests or have a career path that seems interesting to you and in alignment with your career goals.

CLIMBING THE LADDER

Sarah Falls, director of the library at the New York School of Interior Design

In my experience, no professional is an island, and success won't happen in a vacuum. Reaching the next rung on the ladder takes support from colleagues and personal knowledge building. Support comes from well-built networks at work; beyond that, include shareholders whom you support, as well as co-workers and strong mentors in and outside your institution. Don't be afraid to learn from people in terms of knowledge and expertise, but also welcome their constructive criticism.

You must actively seek members for your network, but remember that just "linking them in" online isn't enough. As a librarian starting out 8 years ago, I was lucky to begin my career at a small liberal arts college where librarians, faculty, and staff wore a lot of hats and worked in teams to best help students. I was able to build on a lot of ready-made connections and quickly see the value in them. Some of those connections I maintain today, two jobs later, and use for advice, knowledge, and mentoring. Laying the groundwork early can sustain you throughout your career and at the very least provide you with fun people to see at American Library Association meetings.

Let's explore whom to include in your network. Your job will bring you into contact with those who need your help and service, known as shareholders. First, you can use experiences with them to learn new aspects of your job. I gained new perspectives on the use of images across the humanities for teaching and learning at my first job. As an art librarian, I worked on interesting projects for departments such as Russian, religion, and music and saw how images helped students learn more deeply. The faculty members' gratitude for work done on their behalf led to great friendships, acknowledgments in books and videos, and even lovely presents from other countries. I can call on these shareholders today if I need testimonials on my ability to provide faculty support.

The second set of supporters may be harder to cultivate and requires that you be proactive in finding those in your organization with similar interests and goals. Within a library, there are committees that you can serve on that will bring you into contact with potential supporters, but you should think about ways to connect with members of your information technology (IT) department, educational technology units, and even PR and marketing. If you are in a public library, this might require working across a system and looking at other branches. At my first job, we had a coterie of technology-focused individuals (OK, we were geeks) who lunched together regularly at ethnic restaurants. (If goat wasn't on the menu, it wasn't ethnic enough.) The working friendships we forged were strong ones, and we often made plans for work across departments, as well as learning from one another. Because I was already familiar with the members of this group, it was easy to reach out to them in times of need. I still depend on members of this group to this day to learn about technology trends through their tweets and blogs.

For your final group, identify leaders you look up to and who make you think, "I'd like to be in those shoes one day." Join committees and groups, even if it's just a party-planning committee, that help you make those connections and give you the opportunity to show those you admire what you can do. This will also require moving beyond your work environment to professional organizations, where you should never be shy to volunteer your time and energy. Within these organizations, you'll find new ways to develop your skill sets, gain mentoring opportunities, and make lifelong friends while providing the organization with much-needed fresh ideas and support. I was asked to apply for my second job because of a strong connection I made in my own professional organization, Art Libraries Society of North America (ARLIS/NA). Now in my third job, which is administrative, I have continued not only to gain advice from my ARLIS mentor but also to use what I learned from her on the job in terms of structure, decision making, leadership, and managing employees. From her knowledge of my career and skills, she has provided valuable references during job searches, but even more important, her perspective on a lifelong career helps me frame my own by continually asking myself, Where is it I see myself next? What is it I want to be and what is the path to that place? I couldn't do it without her!

If you would like to develop a mentor relationship with someone you've identified, initiate a conversation and ask whether he or she would be interested in mentoring you. Being asked to be a mentor can be very flattering, but the responsibility can also be time-intensive and shouldn't be entered into lightly. Be professional, and be clear about your needs and expectations. What qualities in the mentor made you seek him or her out? How long do you propose that the mentor relationship last—6 months, 1 year? How often will you talk? Will you meet in person or talk by phone? What do you hope to accomplish together? With any mentor, talk about both your current position and what you aspire to be. The career goals you have outlined should facilitate your conversations about seizing and creating opportunities that will help you achieve your short- and long-term career goals.

Beyond finding a mentor, never stop reading vacancy announcements. Even if you are satisfied with your current position and institution, the responsibilities and qualifications listed in these ads are excellent indicators of trends in the professional marketplace, as well as pathways to your own individual professional growth and development.

Finally, you should have ongoing conversations with your supervisor about your career path and future plans. This can, at times, be tricky. You want to give the impression that you are seeking greater opportunities—without seeking greener pastures. That is, you want your supervisor to know that you have a plan and that you want to grow and learn in your job and in the profession, but you don't want to give the impression that you're ready to jump ship or, even worse, that you've set your sights on your supervisor's job. Be open and honest from the beginning of your employment about being inspired by continuous learning and opportunity; in this way you set the tone of future conversations. The performance appraisal process is another opportunity to talk about what you're doing well, where you would like to develop, and opportunities for the future. Even star performers need to have career ambitions.

Supervisors and Their Employees

American business executive and entrepreneur Harry B. Thayer, who was president and chairman of both Western Electric and AT&T, gave sage advice about the supervisor–employee relationship: "It is easy to fool yourself. It is possible to fool the people you work for. It is more difficult to fool the people you work with. But it is almost impossible to fool the people who work under you."[2]

Stepping Into Management

As part of the survey for this book, we asked respondents about their experience in management and supervisory positions. Of the more than 2,100 respondents, 50 percent said that they were in a management or supervisory position, while 50 percent said they were not. Here is the breakdown:

- Forty-five percent are in a management or supervisory position and want to be.

- Five percent are in a management or supervisory position and *don't* want to be.

- Twenty-four percent are *not* in a management or supervisory position and *don't* want to be.

- Twenty-six percent are *not* in a management or supervisory position but want to be someday.

A PROFILE IN COURAGE

A Q&A with Carol Hunter, deputy university librarian in collections and services at the University of North Carolina–Chapel Hill

Q: Tell us a little bit about your background. How did you get started in libraries?

I earned my MLS in 1978 and spent my first 5 to 7 years in the profession just learning the field. I worked "both sides of the house," meaning I worked in technical services (specifically cataloging) before branching out and moving into research services and reference. I like to say that I have a bit of a "checkered past." I've worked in special libraries and academic libraries as well as for governmental agencies, and I've learned a lot about what all of these libraries have in common. I had my first taste of management when I moved into a position with supervisory responsibilities in 1985.

Q: What was it like moving into a supervisory role and then later into administration?

I don't think I intentionally set out to be in administration; it was just how things progressed. I took advantage of each placement and each position I had, and I was willing to go outside the usual parameters of those positions—I would grab any opportunity I could because I like to make things happen. My first administrative role was as the head of the U.S. Customs Library in New York. It was a very small staff, about five people, and most of the job was doing research for the customs commissioner and managing the other staff. It was a pretty exciting time for technology then, and I introduced new technologies, such as PCs and networking. I also learned firsthand how a team operates and how to get the best out of each person.

Q: What do new administrators need in order to be successful?

To me, administration is about leadership, management, integrity, perseverance, patience, and being positive. When I first started, I needed something to give to people who report to me. I dubbed it "ESP": E for Equip to do the job, S for Support people in their efforts, and P for Prepare for the future. I find this approach to be both practical and an art. I also cannot stress enough the importance of mentorship and "balcony people." If, as Shakespeare says, "All the world's a stage," then we all need people in the balcony cheering for us, people who can see the whole picture and bring others up to see it too. Early in my career, people did this for me. And now, I want to do this for others. I also think there are four things every administrator needs to do:

1. Do your job well. This is the part where perseverance and integrity really matter.
2. Focus on the needs of the entire organization, rather than just yourself.
3. Surround yourself with others who are great at things you don't do well. This builds capacity for the whole team.
4. Be open to opportunity. Stretch yourself beyond the parameters of your current position, and volunteer for everything.

When asked about how prepared they felt for their first management position, approximately 40 percent said they felt prepared and 28 percent said they did not feel prepared. The remaining respondents had not yet held a management position. Several themes emerged from the comments associated with these responses. One was that management courses in library schools are not always sufficient preparation for stepping into management positions. After completing library school, many felt prepared to do the "library work" but not the budgeting, management, or supervision associated with their new professional roles. Many responses indicated that there was no substitute for real-world experience. Some, however, felt prepared to step into management or supervisory positions in libraries because they had management experience in a previous career or had worked in their library for many years in a support staff role.

When you're considering moving into a management position, ask yourself these five questions:[3]

1. Will you be comfortable with having less hands-on responsibility?

2. Can you maintain your poise while enforcing disciplinary guidelines, giving critical performance reviews, and dealing with negativity?

3. Are you willing to acquire skills that you lack in order to be a more effective manager?

4. How confident are you in your ability to make decisions and take responsibility for the outcome?

5. Can you successfully handle the change from friend to boss?

To be ready for the challenge, preparation and a little advance planning are important:

- *Draw on transferable skills.* From previous careers to previous positions, everything you do can prepare you for your first management role. Check out the resource titled "Transferable Skills Sets for Job-Seekers" (www. quintcareers.com/transferable_skills_set.html), which organizes transferable skills into five broad areas: 1) communication; 2) research and planning; 3) human relations; 4) organization, management, and leadership; and 5) work survival skills.[4]

- *Read—a lot.* While not a substitute for personal experience, it's helpful to learn from the experience of others. Check foundational management texts, read articles from scholarly journals and popular magazines, and follow blogs that cover adventures in management and supervision.

- *Talk with people about their personal experiences.* Again, a good mentor can have these conversations with you. So can colleagues who are a little further along in their careers. Work that professional network.

- *Take on increasing challenges.* Perhaps start small, such as leading a committee or managing a project, and then make the move into managing people and resources. The greatest reward for good work is more work. Once you've proven to be reliable, more opportunities (and responsibilities) will come your way.

Dealing With Multiple Generations in the Workplace

There are currently four generations in the workplace:[5] veterans, also known as the silent generation (born between 1922 and 1945); baby boomers (born between 1946 and 1964); Generation X, or Gen Xers (born between 1965 and 1980); and Generation Y, or millennials (born between 1981 and 2000). While each employee is an individual, with his or her own characteristics, work ethic, and communication style, broad generational characteristics have been noted among these groups. Veterans have been described as conformists, with a lot of respect for authority. Baby boomers are characterized by their sense of optimism. Gen Xers grew up as latch-key kids and are said to be fun and informal but also a little skeptical. Lastly, millennials are confident and social, growing up with technology and on-demand services, as well as an "everyone-wins-a-medal" mentality. How do these traits play out in the workplace? Veterans are described as valuing hard work, sacrifice, and rules.

Baby boomers are workaholics and work for personal fulfillment. Gen Xers are self-reliant but also value structure and direction. Millennials are entrepreneurial, goal-oriented, and great at multi-tasking. The key to success for any organization is to effectively channel all these characteristics and to identify when the stereotypes don't fit individuals.

 And the Survey Says ...

There seemed to be common themes in the answers to the question, In terms of generational differences, what's the one thing you want others more junior in the profession to know about you?

- *Remember, I've "been there, done that."*
- *Brains function quite well beyond 30 years of age.*
- *A person's age doesn't necessarily have any relevance to their willingness to accept and adapt to new technology and ideas.*
- *Age doesn't matter; attitude does.*
- *Baby boomers do not like to manage 20-somethings who have been conditioned to believe they are entitled to self-esteem based on nothing. Twenty-somethings must be able to take constructive criticism and seek advice from people who have more experience without feeling grievously offended. They must learn how to attain self-esteem based on real accomplishment and not rely on being excessively stroked and soothed by their managers.*
- *Be nice, honest, patient, respectful, and careful about politics.*
- *Books still have relevant information; it isn't all on the internet.*
- *Don't take on too much debt getting the MLS.*
- *Experience and wisdom come with age.*
- *I worked hard to get where I am.*

- *The reputation I have on campus was earned through a lot of hard work.*
- *I was young once, too.*
- *I am 60, but I am not out of date.*
- *I am here to help you if you need it.*
- *I can be a mentor.*
- *I am not a fuddy-duddy; I am not a dinosaur; I am not dead yet.*
- *I listen to Iron Maiden.*
- *I have strong tech skills, even if I don't have a Facebook page.*
- *Just so you know, I researched all of your social network connections before we even interviewed you.*
- *Even though we might have different personal and individual priorities, I think we share the same overall goals.*

A similarity in answers also occurred in the responses to the question, In terms of generational differences, what's the one thing you want others more senior in the profession to know about you?
- *I care just as much, and being young does not mean that I am not a professional.*
- *Good things can be accomplished without rigid dress codes and with a more relaxed atmosphere. Professionalism isn't just about how one dresses.*
- *I need you as a coach and advocate.*
- *Don't be too stubborn to retire, or the upcoming generation of librarians is going to burn out before getting into the field.*
- *Being able to help you with a job helps me learn.*
- *"Because we have always done it that way" is not a good answer.*
- *We're ready to assume leadership roles. Give us the opportunity.*

- *Just because I'm using computers doesn't mean I plan to replace you with a robot.*
- *Balancing work and family life doesn't make me a less dedicated employee.*
- *I work to live, not the other way around.*
- *I am not tied to an organization as was more common in the past. I prefer to use more technology and work remotely, and I probably won't spend my entire career here. But while I'm here, I will work at 100 percent.*
- *I care about work–life balance and aim for flexibility whenever I can.*
- *Please don't be afraid of technology.*
- *Change is our friend, not our enemy.*
- *I'm not an IT guru just because I'm 10 years younger.*
- *I don't want to steal your job or push you aside. I want to learn from you and work with you—and you have to take me seriously.*
- *I need a strong mentor in my professional life.*
- *Sometimes I feel as if my ideas and enthusiasm are not taken seriously because I am "young."*
- *I may be younger than you, but I can still teach you things.*
- *Don't hoard your knowledge; pass along your tips and tricks.*
- *Tell me if you want me to be formal with you or not. I am happy to oblige; I just can't tell which you prefer.*
- *Retire already! The world won't end. Our generation can handle it. Really.*
- *The number of years of experience does not equal someone being qualified.*
- *I need to feel valued, and I need to feel that my work is meaningful.*
- *It's OK to check Facebook at work.*
- *Innovation can be stifled by the "accepted ways of working"—be open to new ideas.*

- *I have the capacity to lead and manage, but I need opportunities to develop those skills. It's called succession planning.*
- *Introducing new ideas isn't a judgment on how things have been done or a threat to the system.*
- *I may be young but I got this job for a reason: I'm capable.*
- *I'm your peer, not your subordinate.*
- *Since I am the only young person at my job, I want them to understand that I'm lonely.*
- *I'm Gen X, so I straddle the old guard and the new guard in libraries. I often understand where you are coming from and can be a bridge between generations.*
- *Although I'm a millennial, I can take "no" for an answer, get to work on time every day, and work hard without positive reinforcement.*
- *Just because my hair is purple doesn't mean I'm an idiot.*
- *There are some old souls among young librarians.*

From "young" to "old," from millennials to boomers, and everything in between and beyond, we each value who we are and what we have to offer in terms of skills and experience. A word of caution is also heard in some of the comments featured: "Don't write us off" seems to be expressed by a vocal minority, both younger and older. Judge employees based on their technical and professional competence and experience, not by age, perception, or stereotype. Employers should also work to be inclusive of different styles and workplace expectations, reinforcing the fact that we are all stronger when we work together.

Endnotes

1. George T. Doran, "There's a S.M.A.R.T. Way to Write Management's Goals and Objectives," *Management Review* 70, no. 11 (1981): 35.

2. "Harry Bates Thayer (1858–1936)," *ThinkExist.com Quotations Online*, accessed July 10, 2013, thinkexist.com/quotes/harry_b._thayer.

3. Tai Goodwin, "Is Moving to a Management Position Your Next Best Career Move?" *The Career Makeover Coach,* March 16, 2010, accessed July 10, 2013, www.careermakeovercoach.com/is-moving-to-a-management-position-your-next-best-career-move.

4. "Transferable Skills Sets for Job-Seekers," *Quintessential Careers,* accessed July 10, 2013, www.quintcareers.com/transferable_skills_set.html.

5. Greg Hammill, "Mixing and Managing Four Generations of Employees," *FDU Magazine,* winter/spring 2005, accessed July 10, 2013, www.fdu.edu/newspubs/magazine/05ws/generations.htm.

KEEPING UP: FOLLOWING TECHNOLOGY AND TRENDS

Dear Q&A: I guess you could say I'm in the middle of my career. While I'm feeling good about my work, I feel like it is becoming increasingly difficult to stay on top of new technologies and trends. What can I do?

Keeping up is a big part of our jobs and our profession. We are part of a constantly changing and evolving field that is—whether we like it or not—heavily dependent on technology. We need to keep ourselves current, and we need to be aware of (although not necessarily fluent in) the new technologies and trends that may affect our roles, our procedures, and the way in which we find, evaluate, synthesize, classify, and provide access to information. Adopt the mindset that it can be fun to play around with new tools and gadgets, and always think about ways to incorporate new ideas and procedures into your own workplace.

Technology can be both a blessing and a curse. In many ways, we are fortunate to have the tools, resources, and technology of today.

They are things that can inspire, assist, and make our jobs a little easier and significantly more efficient. On the other hand, it takes a lot to keep all these technologies functioning, and as we all know, technologies change—frequently. Whether it's simply an upgraded version or a whole new way of doing things, change is a constant. This can sometimes make us feel like Sisyphus, constantly pushing that boulder up the hill, weighted down by all the new products, devices, resources, concepts, and ideas surrounding us. In this chapter, we emphasize the importance of keeping up, and we outline some ideas for discovering new technologies while increasing your enthusiasm for learning new tools and keeping on top of tech trends.

Keep Up With Technology or Become Obsolete

The need to keep up with new tools and resources or risk becoming obsolete goes back as far as the caveman, as Kevin Fogarty points out: "History shows ... that those who hold on to their own history while that of all the rest of us rushes past them, usually aren't around long enough to hold off an approaching future or reduce our speed toward it."[1]

What New Technology Can Do for You

We can work differently when we start making the shift toward thinking about what technology can do for us and what keeping current can do for our careers.

First, let's focus on what learning new technologies and keeping up with trends can do for you. They can add to your expertise and your skill set and can make you highly marketable and eminently employable. Employers look for candidates who have specific technical skills and are familiar with specific types of software, certain online tools or electronic resources, and emerging trends in the field. Libraries like to use new technologies that will better support their staff and clientele. Every single job within a library uses technology in some way or another; this is an unavoidable component of our profession that we cannot deny, shun, or be afraid of. Many roles in today's libraries are almost entirely technology-based as more and more of our resources are online and more and more of our communication and learning are done online. Why is technology so important? Because it helps us do our jobs better. It helps us create new jobs and find new ways to reach our users. We rely on it for networking, promotion, storage, access, and statistics. We use it to find things. We use it to help others find things. However, technology changes all the time. Before chat reference, we had to exchange emails back and forth and weren't able to "talk" with the patron (in real time) at the other end of the line. Mobile technologies add a new layer of complexity. Just the other day, a colleague referred to both historical markers and the pop-ups on Yelp as "augmented realities"—something that adds information and meaning and can be viewed in the same context as the actual object. This is the world we live in, and it's only getting better. Try to embrace the power of new technologies and find ways to make them work for you. Some define this mind-set as natural curiosity, while others find it more like survival of the fittest. Whatever you call it, just be sure to keep up with what's out there.

Second, be mindful of what you pursue. Yes, just a few sentences ago, we suggested embracing new technologies. That doesn't mean *all* technology. Be selective. Take a careful approach to technology, just as you do with other professional aspects of your life. Take careful stock of what you have and what you know, what serves you well and what needs improvement. Identify the gaps between what you have and what you need (maybe even what you *want*), and find the technology that most helps close that gap. If you're looking for a way to stay in touch with professional colleagues but Facebook isn't your thing, try LinkedIn. Maybe investigate Google+ and set up circles for work friends, professional colleagues, outside vendors, and so on. Think about what you need, and find the right tool for the job. Although you might not dive as deeply in, be sure to keep your head up and your ears open to other products, tools, and services on the market. Hedge your bets. Sometimes we bet wrong and need to make quick adjustments, and that's all right. We learn from failure.

The Law of Accelerating Returns

Ray Kurzweil makes an interesting observation about the rate of technological change:

> *Our forebears expected the future to be pretty much like their present, which had been pretty much like their past. Although exponential trends did exist a thousand years ago, they were at that very early stage where an exponential trend is so flat that it looks like no trend at all. So their lack of expectations was largely fulfilled. Today, in accordance with the common wisdom, everyone expects continuous technological progress and the social repercussions that follow. But the future will be far more surprising than most observers realize: few have truly internalized the implications of the fact that the rate of change itself is accelerating.[2]*

Third, think about the users, the patrons, or the clients of your library. People who use libraries and our services and resources have expectations, needs, and demands. Their technologies are changing, the way they find information is changing, the way they do business is changing, and the way they interact with others is changing. To meet their needs, we must attempt to keep up with them, be slightly ahead of them, or be able to predict where they are going next. A few of the trends that are forcing us to change what we do or how we do things include digital content and digital content devices, mobile technologies, social media communication and marketing, visual information literacy, digital management repositories, cloud computing, distance learning, open source tools and systems, resource sharing, and discovery tools.

Last, think about your colleagues as a team. Your team's goals are to offer better and more user-friendly resources, to expand and adapt existing and new services, and to incorporate new technologies where needed. Think of your library as a place that rewards imagination and encourages experimentation. Keeping up with trends and technology isn't something you do entirely on your own; it should be a team pursuit, one that involves everyone—not just the newest or the youngest or the most adventurous. The quest to always do better usually starts with innovation and an entrepreneurial spirit. "Startup culture is an attitude. It's the responsibility of the administration to foster and inspire the entrepreneurial spirit. It's the role of librarians and staff to push the boundaries, to find what's next, and to redefine our profession."[3]

How to Keep Current

Our survey respondents recommended a number of ways to stay current with new technologies and trends. These are a few of their suggestions:

- Read blogs, discussion lists, tweets, RSS feeds, Google
  alerts, LinkedIn articles, and magazine and journal articles
  (library literature and beyond, specifically *Wired*, *Fast
  Company*, *PC World*, *First Monday*, EDUCAUSE, and
  Chronicle of Higher Education) as well as general news
  sources (newspapers, television, and radio).

- Look outside of the library profession for trends and new
  technologies. The rise of the mobile device has affected
  the way we provide service. What else is out there on the
  marketplace horizon that will change how we operate as a
  library?

- Get experience in person by attending professional
  meetings and conferences, local lectures, and seminars and
  workshops; getting training provided by library vendors;
  networking with and learning from colleagues; and
  pursuing additional coursework or an additional degree (be
  sure to inquire with your current employer about
  educational reimbursements that may help cover tuition
  and fees).

- Learn online by following enewsletters, podcasts, and
  webinars on any number of topics sponsored by
  professional associations; get computer basics from
  GCFLearnFree.org, and listen to inspirational,
  thought-provoking videos from the TED talks series
  (www.ted.com).

Here are a few of our own suggestions to help you stay current:

- Start a monthly meeting for individuals to come together
  to learn more about technology. Each month, one member
  of the group selects an article to share, an app to
  demonstrate, or a new technology to highlight, and
  members discuss applicability for library users and
  services.

- Find or create a technology sandbox, a place where you
  and others can learn and experiment with new
  technologies. Want to learn how to create an online video?

Check out the media center. Want to learn how patrons experience your website on mobile devices? Check out an iPad (or smartphone) and take a look. This is not goofing off; it is research that can have a real impact on the services we provide and how they are delivered.

- Become an app junkie. Experiment with new (and preferably free) apps for your mobile device and see which ones make your life easier, help you stay on top of the latest news, and help keep you organized. Install a new one each week. Keep the few that you actually use; become an "expert" on them and share your experience with your colleagues.

- Identify a group of "early adopters" in your organization and ask them questions. What are they working on? What are they most excited about these days? How do they learn and keep up with new technologies? What are they reading? What apps do they recommend?

- Volunteer to take the lead on a project that will throw you into the realm of new technology. There's nothing more motivating than being held accountable by the many members of your team who are relying on you (and your clever technology skills) to complete the project. If not a specific project, try to identify a personal or professional reason to try something new. Hands-on experience can really supplement what you've read or heard from colleagues and give you firsthand knowledge of how something works.

- Use social media tools to keep informed of what's happening in the profession. Join groups on LinkedIn, "Like" pages on Facebook, and follow people and organizations on Twitter and Google+. You can easily discover and share professional information on these networks (and others) and get quick updates on current trends.

Definition of Librarian

Urban Dictionary *includes the following definition of a librarian:*

A person who is trained to help you find whatever information you might be looking for. Many people have an outdated stereotype of a librarian as an unmarried middle-aged woman who only cares about keeping kids away from her dusty old books. The truth, however, is that librarians come in all shapes, sizes, genders and ages; more important, librarians today are trained in web design, online research (believe it or not, there's far more out there besides Google and Wikipedia), networking, and the latest Web 2.0 technologies. Books are still a huge part of the job, but librarians these days know far more about technology than most people, and are taught exactly how to use it to help you find what you need.[4]

Online Resources

There on many online resources that can help you keep up with technology, trends, and more:

- *ALA TechSource* (www.alatechsource.org) is a unit of the publishing department of the American Library Association (ALA) and generates *Library Technology Reports, Smart Libraries Newsletter*, and the ALA *TechSource Blog.*

- *The Digital Shift* from *Library Journal* (www.thedigital shift.com) is "the new home for all technology-related stories and features published by *Library Journal* and *School Library Journal*. We'll cover everything to keep librarians informed as they help ease patrons' and students' immersion in an increasingly digital world."[5]

- *Google News* (news.google.com) "is a computer-generated news site that aggregates headlines from news sources worldwide, groups similar stories together and displays them according to each reader's personalized interests."[6]

- *Library Technology Guides* (www.librarytechnology.org) "aims to provide comprehensive and objective information related to the field of library automation" and "information on the technology products, companies, and trends that impact libraries."[7]

- *LISNews: Librarian News* (lisnews.org) is a collaborative blog devoted to current events and news in the world of library and information science.

- *TechSoup for Libraries* (www.techsoupforlibraries.org) is a project of TechSoup Global, a nonprofit devoted to making technology and technology education available and affordable to nonprofits and libraries all over the world. It grew out of a desire to specifically address the technology needs of public libraries.

- *Twitter* (twitter.com) "is a real-time information network that connects you to the latest stories, ideas, opinions and news about what you find interesting."[8] Use it as a search engine (twitter.com/search) or create an account to post your own updates, and follow people and groups.

Keeping up with technology and trends can be daunting if you let it overwhelm your professional life. But you shouldn't think of it as a chore; it should be part of your ongoing professional development and a basic requirement of your job—of all our jobs. The more we learn and understand, create and explore, and keep on top of the trends, the better we become at our jobs, at helping our users, and at adding our voices to the discussions that will move our profession into the future. Build a support network in which members learn from each other. Take small steps, and make time in your schedule to play, observe, and learn. Make strategic choices about what to pursue deeply and what to just be aware of. By doing all this, you can put yourself in the driver's seat, making all of it just a little less intimidating.

Endnotes

1. Kevin Fogarty, "Caveman DNA Proves Keeping Up With Technology Is a Survival Tactic," *ITWorld*, April 30, 2012, accessed July 10, 2013, www.itworld.com/it-managementstrategy/273274/caveman-dna-proves-keeping-technology-survival-tactic.

2. Ray Kurzweil, "The Law of Accelerating Returns," *Kurzweil Accelerating Intelligence*, March 7, 2001, accessed July 10, 2013, www.kurzweilai.net/the-law-of-accelerating-returns.

3. Brian Mathews, "Think Like a Startup: A White Paper to Inspire Library Entrepreneurialism," *VirginiaTech: Invent the Future: VTechWorks*, July 10, 2013, accessed July 27, 2012, hdl.handle.net/10919/18649.

4. brianeisley, "Librarian," *Urban Dictionary*, October 4, 2007, accessed July 10, 2013, www.urbandictionary.com/define.php?term=librarian.

5. "About," *The Digital Shift*, accessed April 4, 2013, www.thedigitalshift.com/about.

6. "About Google News," *Google News*, accessed July 10, 2013, www.google.com/intl/en_us/about_google_news.html.

7. "Homepage," *Library Technology Guides*, accessed July 10, 2013, www.library technology.com.

8. "About," *Twitter*, accessed July 10, 2013, twitter.com/about.

COLLABORATION: FORMING
PRODUCTIVE PARTNERSHIPS

Dear Q&A: Time and money are tight, and I feel as if I'm being asked to do more with less. I always think that maybe I could do more with a few partners. Is collaboration the way to go? What can it do for me and my career?

Collaboration is not natural or instinctive for many people. Collaboration takes effort. Successful collaborations also take time, patience, communication, sacrifice, and follow-through, among other things. In just about any industry, collaboration among colleagues, departments, and different institutions is often encouraged, is usually required, and is most likely unavoidable. If done right, collaboration can be extremely beneficial for your career, your professional relationships, your library, and your institution. It requires a commitment between two or more parties to achieve a specific outcome or goal, whether short-term or long-term, finite or ongoing. It is a bond, an agreement, an arrangement, and a process, and it requires organization and planning as well as clearly defined goals and evaluation.

Collaboration can take place on many different levels and in many different partnerships: with a colleague to work on a project or a publication; with other departments or branches in your own institution; with librarians in other libraries; with people or associations or businesses in your community; or with consortia on a local, regional, or national level. Even if your job does not require that you form collaborations, you should seek them out in different forms and see how working with others, and working with people you don't normally work with, can enhance your motivation and your career. Collaboration offers the following benefits, among others:

- Generating and exchanging ideas, perspectives, and viewpoints
- Creating synergy
- Sharing knowledge and workload
- Building friendships
- Reducing costs and duplication of effort
- Proving worth in the community
- Cross-pollinating departments and organizations
- Meeting goals
- Leveraging resources
- Combining knowledge sets
- Solving problems
- Producing energy and motivation
- Learning from others
- Expanding offerings

Collaborate vs. Partner

There are important distinctions between the definitions of collaborate and partner:[1]

Collaborate: *To work jointly on an activity, especially to produce or create something*

Partner: *A person who takes part in an undertaking with another or others, especially in a business or company with shared risks and profits*

Partnering on a Local Level

Partnerships can start out small: just one colleague with another, at the same institution or perhaps a neighboring or sister institution, working on a project, publication, or presentation together or just communicating about a specific challenge or idea. These small-scale collaborations can help form bonds and friendships with colleagues and thus support a better and more productive work environment, at the same time providing professional and open camaraderie with people on the same level as you.

If you work in a library or department that is part of a larger institution, then you are already dependent on other units when it comes to things such as budgets, personnel, information technology, training, building maintenance, and materials processing—or all of the above and more. Sometimes these partnerships are not as amicable as they could be, and sometimes these partnerships are not collaborative in nature. You may not even think of these connections as true partnerships, but it is always a good idea to try to figure out how you can make the relationship both collaborative and productive for all involved. Look into how it can be two-sided (i.e., both sides clearly derive a benefit from it). Are you able to meet in person or online? Perhaps you can form a cross-departmental think tank, library technology committee, or professional development committee with members from various parts of the institution. There are numerous ways to form new collaborations with key people and departments in your institution. What benefits one can benefit all.

Collaboration in a Consortium

Two heads are better than one, as the saying goes. We've all partnered up at some point in our academic or professional lives, and we've all probably had some good experiences and outcomes from our collaborations. Working with others can lighten the load, stimulate ideas, and feed motivation. Librarians and libraries have learned over the years that certain partnerships can be beneficial, especially when it comes to purchasing resources and offering more services to our users as part of a consortium. Library consortia can consist of local, regional, or national associations. Their goals generally revolve around pooling money and expertise in order to coordinate resources and improve services to library users in all types of libraries. As the proverb goes, "Many hands make light work."[2]

A consortium can purchase resources and collections such as databases and books for libraries. It can offer classes, programs, webinars, and vendor demonstrations for librarians. A consortium can coordinate chat and text services across multiple institutions. And consortia can support their members in many other ways. Consortial collaborations make sense for many libraries. After joining, a library becomes part of a larger community, gaining influence as well as access to services and resources it may not have been able to obtain independently.

Collaborating Outside Your Institution

You may collaborate with others within your institution on a daily basis; it may be required of you and may not be that much of a stretch or take that much effort. But when you go outside your institution, outside your comfort zone, you can seek collaborations with colleagues, associations, and libraries that are not dependent on one another and do not answer to the same authority. This type of relationship has the potential to be creative, exciting, dynamic, and advantageous for all involved.

Before you seek collaborations with others outside your institution, you should think about possible ways and reasons to collaborate. In other words, you should have a plan or at least an idea. Do you need (or want) to publish or present but don't want to do it alone? Do you or your department or library have a dilemma that others have already solved? Are you the only person in your library who works with a certain system, technology, or resource and you want to communicate with others who work with it? Are there libraries, schools, or other organizations in your area that you can work with to offer more programs, resources, or services for your community? Are there library consortia that offer services that you need, would make your job easier, or save your library money?

The opportunity to collaborate is yet another reason to build and maintain your professional networks, as discussed in previous chapters. Partnerships and collaborations can be more quickly and easily formed when built on existing relationships. Additionally, collaboration can stretch your skills and experience in new directions, enhancing your resume while expanding your pool of potential employment references.

COLLABORATION ACROSS CONSORTIA

A Q&A with Mona Couts, director of Triangle Research Libraries Network, Chapel Hill, NC

Q: How did you get into libraries?

One summer in college, I talked myself into an internship at a public library. I enjoyed that so much that I majored in library science as an undergrad. After graduation, I worked as an acquisitions librarian at a public library and eventually worked my way up to head of technical services. I knew that I needed an advanced degree to move into higher positions, so I went to Emory University and earned the MLS.

Q: What were your next steps?

I interviewed at the Library of Congress and at a regional public library system in Georgia. I took the public library position because I could participate in a lot of different things, and it recognized my preprofessional experience. I got to build a children's section from the ground up. Later, a friend and I decided to move to Boston. I needed a job and applied for an information consultant position.

Q: The information consultant position must have been very different from working in a public library. What's the best advice you can give to people considering a career as an information consultant?

Consultant work is like solving a big puzzle. You need to come in, quickly learn what's going on, and be prepared to offer solutions. You also don't have to stick around to implement anything, so it's a lot of analysis and decision making, without implementation. But the best advice is this: When you get off the airplane, go to the bathroom. Because they are paying so much for your time, businesses never build in bathroom breaks!

Q: After consultant work, what was next?

I left consulting to work for Blackwell Library Systems. It was developing a serials and acquisitions management system. After I completed 6 weeks' training in Oxford, the first two U.S. customers were New York Public and University of California–Berkeley, both dramatically different from the European customers, which were primarily small pharmaceutical companies. After 4 years, U.S. operations were closed down, and I went to work for one of the former Blackwell customers here in the U.S. as the head of systems for a health sciences library on an academic campus. I could have gone to work for another vendor, but I wanted to try working in a library again and wanted less travel. I gradually built up the staff of the library systems department and was promoted to assistant director over several departments. But I discovered that I preferred the type of position in which I can start things and manage projects, not necessarily spend a lot of time on implementation. When a position became available as an information technology program officer at Triangle Research Libraries Network (TRLN; www.trln.org), I thought it would be a great opportunity to work with a lot of different libraries on a lot of different things.

Q: You then moved into the director's position at TRLN. What's life like at a consortium?

I've always believed in collaboration, and at TRLN, I get to work on great projects with the best and brightest library staff, who are committed to doing great things together. I'm also a real process queen—I like to organize and figure out the best structures, who needs to be involved, and how to make people feel as if they're contributing and involved members of that process. I like to get good people around a table to accomplish good things—more than they could do by themselves, something to be proud of.

Q: What does someone need in order to be successful as the director of a consortium?

First, you need to develop credibility in order to be successful. You have to consistently deliver a quality product. You need to have no ego. You can't waste people's time. You need to be comfortable taking orders from a lot of other people and be able to nudge from behind. When dealing with multiple library directors (as at TRLN), it is important that I know their individual vision and priorities. I am really a generalist; I know a little bit about a lot. It's important to know people and how to work with them to cultivate relationships at all levels. And most of all, always enjoy what you do, do fun stuff, and find fun people to work with.

Finding Partners to Collaborate With

When you attend meetings, classes, symposia, or conferences, whether locally or nationally, you should always try to meet and talk to new people. If you are attending these events, you presumably have interests, roles, or goals similar to those of the other attendees. Strike up conversations, collect contact information, and follow up with the people you meet.

Locate and get involved in existing groups or associations, which are natural venues for finding potential partners, sharing information, and asking questions. Look for in-person meetings of local associations or special interest groups (library and nonlibrary) and for online groups that are active on LinkedIn, Facebook, or Twitter. If you have specific ideas for collaborative projects, put them out there. Send out requests to the group, to email lists, or on social media sites, and see who responds.

If you want to work in groups with other libraries or with library departments in other institutions, speak first to your supervisor or director and see whether there is a history of collaboration among the groups. If it's a case of collaboration that did not go well in the past, you still can try again. See if you can organize a joint meeting. Keep it focused on one or two concepts or initiatives. Have an agenda, and then keep up with communication. Just speaking with others in similar libraries or roles can generate great ideas and provide motivation and allies.

Collaboration may allow you to attain a goal or achieve a certain status that you couldn't reach on your own. It might allow you to offer more services and resources for your users. It might be a way to effect change, promote progress, or advance ideas at another level. Collaboration is a skill and a mind-set. Once you get good at it, after lots of practice, you should be able to easily form new collaborations and identify new partnerships on an ongoing basis. You may even discover that, after you've been involved in successful collaborations and developed successful partnerships with other librarians and organizations, they will find you—even when you aren't looking for them.

 And the Survey Says ...

Here is a selection of responses to, The best thing about collaboration is ... :

- *Getting the library brand out there in a positive way. Libraries need to prove their worth to their community now more than ever.*
- *Collaboration means different points of view and people who might see things that I am simply overlooking. I have had many aha! moments just by having a team meeting and getting input from my co-workers.*

- *The best thing about collaboration is knowing that I am not alone with my dilemma. I have professionals whom I can call on for their expertise, which increases my self-confidence, and I also make myself available to others.*
- *Collaboration with other organizations makes it easier for me to sell my ideas to the people in my organization who matter.*
- *It fills in the holes in my ideas and can often scale up a plan that's too small potatoes or rein in a crazy idea that's too grandiose.*
- *It brings to light different ways to look at an issue and innovative solutions for various problems. It also can open doors for funding that may not have been available for one institution alone or open doors for smaller institutions to take part in more expensive projects (e.g., digitization or content management) because they can pool resources.*
- *Collaboration has been very rewarding. I've participated in some group presentations and writing projects that I would never have dared on my own.*
- *I like the adage that's been adopted by the hydra project: "If you want to go fast, go alone. If you want to go far, go together." Projects developed with others tend to have better outcomes and more staying power.*

Endnotes

1. "Partner," *Oxford Dictionaries*, accessed April 4, 2013, oxforddictionaries.com/definition/english/partner?q=partner, and "Collaborate," *Oxford Dictionaries*, accessed July 10, 2013, oxforddictionaries.com/definition/english/collaborate?q=collaborate.
2. John Heywood, *Wikiquote*, accessed July 10, 2013, en.wikiquote.org/wiki/John_Heywood.

$Q\&A$
14

RETIREMENT: WRAPPING UP YOUR CAREER AND PLANNING FOR THE NEXT STAGE

Dear Q&A: I am approaching a real milestone! With mixed emotions, I'm thinking about retirement. What do I need to know? And how should I prepare?

Retirement is something we will all face. It is a natural part of our careers, the final stage of our professional working lives, and the wrapping up of the accumulation of experience, skills, successes, and challenges that have defined our careers. Although retirement may represent the culmination of a professional working life, it does not have to signify an end of one's involvement in the profession or an end to one's passion, motivation, and commitment as a professional. Retirement is not a bad word, nor is it something to fear, deny, or ignore (as in, not plan for). We should all be thinking ahead and planning for retirement because, before we know it, the time will arrive.

Ideally, you should start thinking about and planning for retirement years before it actually happens. In today's economic environment, some people are working more years than they anticipated because they can't afford to retire. But we are also seeing the opposite: People being "eased" into retirement because of severe budget cuts. In light of unpredictable events and economic uncertainties, we really do need to start thinking and planning well ahead of time. You never know what may happen with your position, your institution, or your financial portfolio in the future.

Preparing Others

If you've worked in the same library or institution for many years, then you have built up memories about many aspects of the job: your position, the positions and roles around you, the processes and procedures, the progress and setbacks you've encountered, and the way the library and the institution work and run. This is called *organizational memory* (sometimes called *institutional* or *corporate memory*), which may be defined as follows:

> the accumulated body of data, information, and knowledge created in the course of an individual organization's existence. Falling under the wider disciplinary umbrella of knowledge management, it has two repositories: an organization's archives, including its electronic databases; and individuals' memories.[1]

Organizational memory includes loads of accumulated knowledge and information—more than you realize—that you may or may not have been documenting along the way. Whether you care to think of yourself as one, you (yes, you) are a *knowledge management resource*. You have contributed to the organizational memory of the institution. Before you leave, you should document what you've learned, what you remember, and what you have reflected on during your career and the time you've spent at a particular institution. This documentation will help you plan your exit and develop training materials for your library and for your replacement.

In our survey, 12 percent of respondents said they were considering retirement in the next 1 to 3 years, and 17 percent said they do not expect their organization to fill their position when they retire. Many libraries leave positions unfilled when someone leaves, while others rework a vacated role into something different. Even if you know you will not be replaced when you retire, you should document and prepare training materials. Someone will be taking over your responsibilities and carrying on some of your procedures. Every librarian has a unique job, set of skills, and way of doing things. The longer you have been in a certain role or library, and the longer you've been doing the same tasks, the more you have honed your processes and figured out how to do your work in the best way possible (for you anyhow). This may not be the best way for someone else, and it may not even be the most efficient or productive or innovative way, but you don't have to worry about that—just document what you do and how you do things, and let others figure out what to do with that knowledge once you are gone.

Libraries undergo constant change. Our roles change, our systems change, our procedures change, and our patrons change. It can be tiring to keep up with all this change and stay current, motivated, and involved. As we near retirement, it might be easy to avoid change or to refuse to change because "What's the point, I'm out of here soon anyway." It might be difficult to focus on changes inside the institution when you are focusing on other things, such as financial planning and what you are going to do after you retire. However, as long as you are "on the job," you should attempt to stay involved in your role and the daily procedures and to contribute to discussions, planning, and new projects. Doing these things will keep you energized and help your colleagues stay connected to you as they benefit from your knowledge, advice, ideas, and history with the institution.

We urge those facing imminent retirement to remain engaged in the life and evolution of their library, to document their organizational memory, and to communicate with those around them, lest the library suffer when they leave. No matter how you may feel about leaving, and even if your library does not replace you, your role (and your legacy) is important, and you should be proud of all that you have accomplished. So be sure to take ownership of your career, especially at the end of it, rather than leave a black hole behind you.

And the Survey Says ...

Respondents provided some very wise advice when asked, What advice would you give to others who will consider retirement in the next few years?

- *If you are healthy and still having fun at work, don't retire yet!*
- *Make sure that your job is not your life. If you have no other interests, get some!*
- *Figure out what is important to you, what you must have, and what you can do without. Also, what are your interests outside work? If you have few or none, start developing some, or you will find retirement is not a happy time.*
- *Phase out your work gradually.*
- *Prepare for it as you would a new job.*
- *Work with a financial planner and make a list of the 10 things you want to do most.*
- *Keep reading and consulting with professionals. Keep current and prepare to reinvent yourself.*
- *Start planning now, not only financially but also emotionally and psychologically. It's a big step!*

- *Practice living now on what your likely income will be in the future—and put the difference into savings.*
- *Never coast—even during the last 6 months. You're only as relevant as your most recent project. Share your visions and expertise with others on your staff.*
- *Make your decision when you are ready. Don't let others pressure you into retiring. Be sure that it is your choice, that you want it, and that you are ready for it.*
- *Work as if you won't retire. Plan work for after you retire—even if it is housework. Cultivate social connections you may have neglected while working. Live on half your salary.*
- *The skills you have developed as a librarian can be applied to myriad volunteer opportunities, and the intellectual curiosity that is a prerequisite for all librarians will mean that you are never bored.*
- *Don't coast simply because you are close to retirement. Do your job to the best of your ability, and enjoy the relationships you have as a result of your job. Continue those relationships after you retire.*
- *Be sure you're grooming staff to operate without you and to be ready for change.*

Preparing Yourself

The decision to retire (and the reasons for retiring) is different for each person. You may be ready emotionally but not financially, or vice versa. Likewise, there is no magic age for retirement, even though you might have a number in your head. It is up to you, your family, your resources, and your employer to determine when it is your time. And just as you prepared for your entrance into your career by going to school, developing goals, honing skills, exploring different roles, building relationships, and forming collaborations, you will need to prepare for your exit from your career. Both processes can be exciting and intimidating, and a little scary. And both require lots and lots of planning.

Financial planning is crucial. Depending on where you have worked and how long, you may have built up a comfortable savings in a retirement or pension plan. Before you retire, you will need to figure out how far that money will go and think about expected and unexpected expenses, such as healthcare, housing, travel, inflation, and other personal factors that will undoubtedly eat into your funds. Many employers provide access to investment advisors and offer classes or workshops on retirement planning. Take advantage of these while you are still working or seek financial advice so that you can create an actual plan for your financial future postretirement. You should develop your plan with your spouse and other family members who may be affected by it. Start creating your plan several years before you retire if at all possible so that you can live with it for a while, make changes to it if needed, and think about how you will use it to pave the way to an enjoyable and stress-free retirement.

TALES OF A RETIREE

A Q&A with Valerie Feinman, retired librarian and former coordinator for instruction at Adelphi University, Long Island, NY

Q: What's your story?

I began paying into a retirement fund in 1964, when I was on the faculty at Syracuse. I didn't think much about it, but I stayed with it throughout my career, and I persuaded my spouse to enter the same system when he began working for a nonprofit in 1969. We had two kids, bought a house, and continued our careers. He retired in the late 1990s, and I followed suit a few years later. In

2006, he was diagnosed with a terminal illness, and we knew we didn't have much time left together. Throughout his illness, he strongly encouraged me to keep active in my profession, to write about it, and to attend conferences. He said to me many times, "Librarianship is your life and it remains your 'sanity support system'—carry on with it after I'm gone." And so I have. It is weird, and lonely, to return home after a conference and find that he is not there for a discussion of trends and events.

Q: What advice can you give to retirees or those about to retire?

Think ahead about the sort of life you wish to lead. You may wish to move closer to grandkids or to embrace athletic activities. Remember that you are growing older and that your body may slow down. Find an exercise or a swimming class, or a ping pong, bridge, or mah-jongg group. Join a book club. Find excuses to get out of your house or apartment several times each week. Form a kaffeeklatsch of other about-to-retire library people, and discuss all these opportunities.

Think about where all your favorite doctors, therapists, and dentists are located. I could not move far from my current location and be happy with the medical help I need as I age. I am growing older, and can't stop the process. Osteoarthritis—ouch!

Query your professional societies, many of which are developing retirement round tables (RMRTs); help by proofreading bylaws and archival materials or by writing for blogs and newsletters. Get involved in an oral history group. Work on the archives of your local library. Think about continuing activities within the American Library Association (ALA) itself. Do you know that after 25 years of professional ALA membership, you become a lifetime member and do not need to pay dues? Think about attending conferences, particularly those close to home, and take advantage of virtual committee membership.

Offer yourself as a mentor. Librarians climbing up the promotional ladder often wish to talk to a librarian who is not from their shop. Someone within your previous library may also need some advice; at least take him or her out for coffee and discuss professional development or tenure issues.

Think ahead about holidays ... and plan not to be alone. There are always local groups or friends you could ask, or you could travel to meet a friend somewhere. Nearby me, there is a very charming old church where my neighbors gather for caroling at Christmas. I try to always attend and sing along. Birthdays can be lonely. I realized recently that since 1978, when I joined ALA, I have been at ALA more often than at home on my birthday (in late June). I have a group of librarian friends with whom I celebrate, often in an Irish pub, on that day.

Q: How have you stayed active in the profession?

I have continued to attend ALA and Association of College and Research Libraries conferences. I have joined my state library association, and I attend local conferences. I participate in a mentoring program for academic librarians, and I write articles for a librarian newsletter. I was appointed an emerita member of LIRT, where I have been a member since1983. I was named a Nassau County Scholar and then asked to reorganize the library of the County Planning Committee. I was named a director of both the Friends of the Adelphi Library and the Great Neck Historical Society. I was an early interviewee for the Capturing Our Stories project (an oral history program of retiring and retired librarians), and I prepared the first RMRT program for an ALA national conference based on that project. I am currently writing the introduction to a new book about the history of librarianship, and I continue to collect pages for my autobiography, *Sixty Years in the Stacks*, and hope to finish it within the year. I also tend to my family and make quilts.

Retiring from your career is different from quitting a job or moving into another role. It is a major life event, and it should be treated as such. Prepare yourself for the emotional impact it will have on your life. Don't leave until the last minute things such as cleaning up your office and connecting with colleagues. Give yourself time to reflect on your career and to enjoy the final months, weeks, and days in your job. Susan Carol Curzon writes about retiring graciously in *Pre- & Post-Retirement Tips for Librarians.* "To retire graciously means that we retire in a manner that is respectful of our colleagues, our library, our profession, and ourselves. The process of retiring from the library is often our final professional act. Retiring graciously is a statement about how much we cared about our library and our profession."[2]

Everyone's professional journey is different, everyone's career choices are different, and everyone's experiences are different. It's the same with retirement. Maybe you've asked yourself, "What will I do with myself if I retire?" Perhaps you haven't given it much thought, or you think you will revel in doing nothing all day (and maybe you will). However, based on all the advice available about retirement and achieving personal contentment after you stop working, we recommend that you plan on doing something. Typically, for most people, retirement doesn't mean waiting to die. It means a new beginning and a newfound appreciation for things you haven't had time to appreciate. Retirement is a goal and an accomplishment.

Hobbies can go a long way toward keeping you busy. Cooking, gardening, reading, writing, sewing, traveling, swimming, cycling, organizing, walking, kayaking, birding, and painting are all excellent and potentially rewarding ways to stay active, entertained, and engaged. There are also plenty of group activities that can provide you with adult conversation and social interactions; examples include book clubs, writing groups, recreational groups, fitness clubs, online social networks, spiritual groups, political organizations, and classes of any kind.

If you want to stay involved in the profession (and you should, at least a little), you can maintain your memberships in associations (the good news is that you now pay the retired-member rate, which can represent a substantial reduction). You can attend conferences, symposia, events, and classes because you have more time to do so. You can meet colleagues for lunch and visit libraries you didn't have time to visit before. You can write that article you've been thinking about, start a blog, volunteer, speak or present on a variety of topics (retirement being one of them), get a part-time job, or freelance as a consultant. You can do any number of things. You can use your skills and your experience in any number of ways. You can embark on new adventures. You can enjoy your accomplishments. You can reinvent yourself. You can start again. You can relax and get ready, because the next act is just beginning.

THOUGHTS ON THE RETIREMENT EXPERIENCE

A Q&A with Jenifer Abramson, assistant director for academic human resources at the University of California–Los Angeles Library

Q: Tell us about yourself.

I worked as a librarian in law, lab school, and academic libraries and in several functional areas before I moved into human resources. I welcomed the opportunity to coach and mentor the next generation(s) of librarians, and to help build and improve the infrastructure for learning and development, peer review, and recruitment for my library.

I have enjoyed having as a colleague and friend the director of my campus retiree center. For the past 2 years, she has included me in the programming she arranged for her constituents, namely, retired campus employees and faculty. One important thing I learned is that one must plan for retirement in several ways: the psychological and emotional aspects as well as the financial part.

Q: What will you do after you retire?

I have heard this question many times since my retirement was first announced 8 months ago. Some who asked were simply curious. I think that others asked as a way to start "trying on" retirement: *What would I do if I could retire today?*

Friends who retired before me have offered helpful advice: Don't feel pressured to make a lot of plans. Give yourself time to realize fully that you don't have to be anywhere at a certain time—that is, unless you want to.

What will I do after I retire? is a fundamentally important question. It takes longer to answer it well and fully than I ever expected, but here's what I have learned:

- Give yourself and your employer time to prepare for your departure. Set an exit date 6 to 9 months or more in advance, if you can.
- Count the days toward retirement. Literally. It will provide focus, create a sense of urgency, and build excitement.
- Be prepared to see your to-do list grow as your target date approaches.

As I engaged with the reality of retirement, I saw the question change. It became, progressively, *What do I want to do?* If you find this difficult to imagine, start with these steps:

- *Day 1*: Go for a walk. Clear weeds from a patch in the yard. Read a book (most of us have a stack of books to read "someday"). Take a nap.
- *Week 1*: De-clutter one drawer or one shelf in the guest room, garage, or shed. Have coffee or tea with a different neighbor every other day. Choose something from your Day 1 list.

- *Month 1*: Set a date for lunch with a friend you have not seen in months or years. Gather clothes, kitchenware, and so on, and take them to a charity. Choose books you have enjoyed and register them on a book sharing site (e.g., Book Crossings). Design a book plate, add one to each book, and share them with others.

Another question that comes up is, *Who will I be in retirement?* Few people talk about the necessary identity shift, but the following thoughts might arise:

- I am "known" by my business card. Does it matter that I will not have one? How will I let others know how to reach me? Perhaps I should design a card for my "retired self."
- How can I still be valuable? Is it enough that family or friends value me? Maybe I can help to nurture the next generation by caring for and reading to my grandchildren and my great nieces and nephews.
- If I want to do more, how do I want to contribute? What do I like to do? For example, if I love to read aloud, maybe I can approach a local hospital (or skilled nursing facility or church or school) and offer to read to a person or group each week. I also enjoy engaging with others around books, so perhaps I can invite my friends to join me in a book discussion group. I find satisfaction in pulling weeds, so I can offer to weed the garden of a friend or neighbor who can no longer do so (or hates to do it).

Consider moving from being goal-driven, defined or confined by time, toward ... something new.

Endnotes

1. "Organizational Memory," *Wikipedia*, accessed July 10, 2013, en.wikipedia.org/wiki/Organizational_memory.

2. Susan Carol Curzon, "How to Retire Graciously," in *Pre- & Post-Retirement Tips for Librarians*, ed. Carol Smallwood (Chicago, IL: American Library Association, 2012), 21.

Appendix **A**

CONTRIBUTORS

We are so very grateful for everyone who provided their expertise to the "Voice of Experience" sidebars in this book. It wouldn't be the same without their personal stories and advice, and we hope you agree.

Jenifer Abramson, assistant director for academic human resources at the UCLA Library

Laura Blessing, director of personnel management at North Carolina State University Libraries

Billy Cook, 2012 MLS graduate of the School of Information and Library Science at the University of North Carolina at Chapel Hill

Lisa Chow, People Interact Consultancy

Mona Couts, director of Triangle Research Libraries Network, Chapel Hill, NC

Suzanne Crow, library director at The Spence School, New York, NY

Sarah Falls, director of the library at the New York School of Interior Design

Valerie Feinman, retired librarian and former coordinator for instruction at Adelphi University, Long Island, NY

Caroline Fuchs, associate professor and outreach librarian at St. John's University, New York, NY

Naomi House, founder, publisher, and editor of I Need a Library Job

Carol Hunter, deputy university librarian for collections and services at the University of North Carolina at Chapel Hill

Ellen Mehling, job bank manager and career development consultant at the Metropolitan New York Library Council, and director of internships for Long Island University's Palmer School of Library and Information Science

Richard A. Murray, metadata librarian at Duke University Libraries and assistant editor of LIScareer.com

Sandra Sajonas, People Interact Consultancy

Laura Schimming, information and education services librarian at the Mount Sinai School of Medicine, New York, NY

Pam Sessoms, LibraryH3lp.com

Priscilla K. Shontz, editor for LIScareer.com

Carrie Netzer Wajda, new business librarian at Y&R, New York, NY

Jennifer L. Ward, information technology services employee at University of Washington Libraries

Appendix **B**

Resources

Books

Arruda, William, and Kirsten Dixson. 2007. *Career Distinction: Stand Out by Building Your Brand*. Hoboken, NJ: Wiley.

Bratter, Bernice, and Helen Dennis. 2008. *Project Renewment: The First Retirement Model for Career Women*. New York: Scribner.

Covey, Stephen R. 2004. *The 7 Habits of Highly Effective People: Restoring the Character Ethic*. New York: Free Press.

De Stricker, Ulla, and Jill Ann Hurst. 2011. *The Information and Knowledge Professional's Career Handbook: Define and Create Your Success*. Oxford, UK: Chandos.

Dority, G. Kim. 2012. *LIS Career Sourcebook: Managing and Maximizing Every Step of Your Career*. Westport, CT: Libraries Unlimited.

———. 2006. *Rethinking Information Work: A Career Guide for Librarians and Other Information Professionals*. Westport, CT: Libraries Unlimited.

Doucett, Elisabeth. 2011. *What They Don't Teach You in Library School*. Chicago: American Library Association.

Gordon, Rachel Singer. 2006. *The Nextgen Librarian's Survival Guide*. Medford, NJ: Information Today.

———. 2008. *What's the Alternative? Career Options for Librarians and Info Pros*. Medford, NJ: Information Today.

Lankes, R. David. 2011. *The Atlas of New Librarianship*. Cambridge, MA: MIT Press.

Lawson, Judy, Joanna Kroll, and Kelly Kowatch. 2010. *The New Information Professional: Your Guide to Careers in the Digital Age*. New York: Neal-Schuman.

Lowell, Laura. 2011. *#My Brand Tweet (Book01). A Practical Approach to Building Your Personal Brand*. Cupertino, CA: THiNKaha.

Newlen, Robert R. 2006. *Resume Writing and Interviewing Techniques That Work: A How-to-Do-It Manual for Librarians*. New York: Neal-Schuman.

Pressley, Lauren. 2009. *So You Want to Be a Librarian!*. Duluth, MN: Library Juice Press.

Schawbel, Dan. 2009. *Me 2.0: Build a Powerful Brand to Achieve Career Success*. New York: Kaplan.

Shontz, Priscilla K., and Richard A. Murray. 2007. *A Day in the Life: Career Options in Library and Information Science*. Westport, CT: Libraries Unlimited.

———. 2012. *What Do Employers Want? A Guide for Library Science Students*. Santa Barbara, CA: Libraries Unlimited.

Smallwood, Carol. 2012. *Pre- & Post-Retirement Tips for Librarians*. Chicago: American Library Association.

Smallwood, Carol, and Rebecca Tolley-Stokes. 2012. *Mentoring in Librarianship: Essays on Working With Adults and Students to Further the Profession*. Jefferson, NC: McFarland.

Tucker, Cory, and Reeta Sinha. 2006. *New Librarian, New Job: Practical Advice for Managing the Transition*. Lanham, MD: Scarecrow Press.

Wallace, Martin, Rebecca Tolley-Stokes, and Erik Sean Estep. 2011. *The Generation X Librarian: Essays on Leadership, Technology, Pop Culture, Social Responsibility and Professional Identity*. Jefferson, NC: McFarland.

Online Resources

ALA JobLIST, joblist.ala.org

ALA TechSource, www.alatechsource.org

Ask a Manager, www.askamanager.org

Capturing Our Stories: Developing a National Oral History Program for Retiring/Retired Librarians, www.ischool.utexas.edu/~stories

Career Q&A with the Library Career People, librarycareer people.com

FlexJobs, www.flexjobs.com

Hiring Librarians, hiringlibrarians.com

INALJ (I Need a Library Job), inalj.com

Library Worklife: HR E-News for Today's Leaders, ala-apa.org/ newsletter

LIScareer.com, www.liscareer.com

Open Cover Letters: Anonymous cover letters from hired librarians & archivists, opencoverletters.com

People Interact, peopleinteract.wordpress.com

Reach Personal Branding, www.reachpersonalbranding.com

Stephen R. Covey, www.stephencovey.com/7habits/7habits.php

Toastmasters International, www.toastmasters.org/tips.asp

Appendix **C**

Survey

Career Q&A: Managing a Successful Career in Librarianship

Introduction and Welcome

Welcome to the Career Q&A career transitions survey. We're gathering this data in preparation for our forthcoming publication on managing a successful career in libraries. We're collecting responses from librarians working in all types of libraries at all stages of their careers on a wide range of topics.

We anticipate the survey will take 10–20 minutes to complete, and individual responses will be anonymous. There are no foreseeable risks associated with this survey, and the confidentiality of your responses will be protected.

We're aiming for a large number of responses, so please feel free to share this survey with colleagues—all responses are welcome and valuable.

Demographic Information, Pt. 1

1. Do you have an MLS or equivalent?

Yes

No

If Yes, what year did you earn the degree?

2. How many years of experience do you have as a professional librarian?

0–5

6–10

11–15

16–20

20+

I have not held a professional librarian position.

3. Have you ever worked in a library support staff position?

Yes

No

4. Are you currently employed in a position that requires an MLS?

Yes

No

5. Do you see benefits of having the MLS?

Yes

No

If Yes, please describe what you believe them to be.

6. In what type of library are you currently employed?

Academic

Public

School

Special

Other

I'm not currently employed in a library.

If Other, please describe.

Demographic Information, Pt. 2

7. Do you currently work full-time or part-time?

Full-time

Part-time

8. How many total staff, including librarians, are in your library?

Fewer than 10

10–30

31–100

More than 100

9. How many librarians work in your library?

Fewer than 10

10–20

21–50

More than 50

Demographic Information, Pt. 3

10. Your gender

Female

Male

Other/Prefer not to answer

11. Your age

   20–29

   30–39

   40–49

   50–59

   60–69

   70+

12. What was your undergraduate degree discipline?

   Arts

   Humanities

   Physical/Natural/Life Sciences

   Social Sciences

13. What was your undergraduate major?

14. Other than the MLS, do you have additional graduate degrees?

   Yes

   No

   If Yes, please specify level of degree.

15. Please select the state or province where you are currently working.

Experience With Hiring

16. Have you ever participated in the hiring or search committee process for a professional librarian position?

   Yes

   No

17. What one piece of advice would you give to a candidate creating a resume?

18. What one piece of advice would you give to a candidate writing a cover letter?

19. What type of information do you find essential on a resume?

20. What's the worst thing you've seen on a candidate's resume?

21. What type of information do you find essential in a cover letter?

22. What's the worst thing you've seen in a candidate's cover letter?

Recently Hired

23. Have you interviewed or started a new job in the last two years?
    Yes
    No

24. What's the best advice you could pass along to someone currently on the job market?

25. What type of resource helped you find the vacancy announcement for your position? (Check all that apply)
    Listserv
    Print resource
    Website
    Word of mouth
    Other
    If you selected Other, please specify:

26. If you had a telephone interview, how did you prepare for it?

27. What advice would you give to others preparing for a telephone interview?

28. If you had an in-person interview, how did you prepare for it?

29. What advice would you give to others preparing for an in-person interview?

Management and Supervisory Positions

30. Are you in a management or supervisory position?
    Yes, and I want to be.
    Yes, and I don't want to be.
    No, and I don't want to be.
    No, but I want to be someday.

31. Did you feel prepared for your first management position?
    I've not been in a management position.
    Yes, I felt prepared for my first management position.
    No, I did not feel prepared for my first management position.

32. What advice would you give to someone coming into his/her first management position?

33. My current library provides sufficient opportunity to move into leadership or management positions.
    Strongly Agree
    Agree
    Disagree
    Strongly Disagree

34. In order to move into a leadership or management position, I will need to look at libraries other than my own.
Strongly Agree
Agree
Disagree
Strongly Disagree

35. What makes a good leader?

36. What makes a good manager?

Professional Activity

37. Are you professionally active in local, state, national or international professional associations? (Check all that apply)
Local
State
National
International
I'm not professional active.
Other
If you selected Other, please specify.

38. How did you first get started with professional activity? (Check all that apply)
I'm not professionally active.
Colleague referral
Sought it out on my own
Supervisor recommendation
Stumbled into it
Other
If you selected Other, please specify:

39. Do you see benefits to participating in professional activity?
Yes
No
If Yes, please describe what you believe them to be.

40. What advice would you give to other librarians considering professional service and activity?

41. Did your professional activity ever result in a new job, professional opportunity or career advancement?
Yes
No
If Yes, please describe.

Career Transitions

42. What advice would you give to someone wanting to switch from one type of library/role to another?

43. What skills are most transferable from one type of library/role to another?

44. If you were to look for a position outside of libraries where you could utilize your skills and your MLS degree, what would it be?

45. Have you recently experienced a major life event, such as the birth or adoption of a child, caring for an elderly parent, or serious illness?
Yes
No
If Yes, please describe what you believe them to be.

46. What arrangements did you make with your employer to adjust your professional responsibilities to accommodate these major life events?

47. Do you feel librarianship is a career option that supports a healthy work–life balance?
Yes
No

48. Do you feel your employer supports a healthy work–life balance?
Yes
No

49. Have you had the need or opportunity to reinvent your role or responsibilities?
Yes
No
If Yes, please describe.

50. How do you learn about and explore new trends and technologies?

Generations in the Workplace

51. Do you feel ageism (preference given to a particular age group) exists in libraries?
Yes
No

52. In terms of generational differences, what's the one thing you want others more JUNIOR in the profession to know about you?

53. In terms of generational differences, what's the one thing you want others more SENIOR in the profession to know about you?

Preparing for Retirement

54. Are you considering retirement in the next 1 to 3 years?
Yes
No

55. What factors weigh most heavily in your consideration? (Check all that apply)
Burnout/boredom on the job
Finances
Institutional pressure to retire
Personal obligations
Other
If you selected Other, please specify:

56. When you retire, do you expect your organization to fill your position?
Yes
No

57. In what ways has your organization helped you prepare for retirement? (Check all that apply)
Employer-supplemented retirement plans
Financial planning classes or workshops
Organizational support
Phased retirement option
Retirement incentives
No assistance has been provided
Other
If you selected Other, please specify:

58. What advice would you give to others who will consider retirement in the next few years?

Forming Partnerships and Collaboration

59. In terms of your professional relationships, how do you identify potential partnerships and collaborations?

60. In your experience, what's been the best thing about collaboration?

61. How do you stay motivated on the job?

Conclusion

Thank you so much for your time and your feedback. Your answers will be valuable as we compile the data for our forthcoming publication on library career transitions and managing a successful career in libraries.

62. Is there anything else you would like to tell us?

63. (OPTIONAL) We'll be using some of these responses in our forthcoming publication. If you would like your quotes attributed, enter your first name and the first initial of your last name.

Thank you again for your time and responses.

About the Authors

Susanne Markgren is the digital services librarian at Purchase College, State University of New York. Previously, she worked in public libraries, a theater library, a government library, a seminary library, a university library system, and a medical school library. Susanne has held responsibilities (some concurrently) in interlibrary loan, reserves, access services, cataloging, reference and instruction, web development, and systems and electronic resources. She is a past president of the Greater New York Metropolitan Chapter of the Association of College and Research Libraries and continues to serve on the executive board. She received her BA from the University of Wisconsin–Eau Claire and her MLIS from the University of Texas at Austin. In her spare time (or because she just might be insane), she is completing a master of fine arts, teaching a for-credit information literacy class, coordinating a mentoring program, serving as a mentor, writing a career column, helping to plan conferences, designing logos and websites, trying to figure out this

Twitter thing, remodeling a house, raising three kids ... and still wondering, what's next?

Tiffany Eatman Allen is the director of Library Human Resources at the University of North Carolina–Chapel Hill. She has worked in libraries for more years than she's willing to admit, including in the catalog department of an academic library, the library of a pharmaceutical company, and a private biomedical research foundation library. This adventure all started with a job in the City and Regional Planning Library as an undergraduate student employee. She received her BA and MLS from the University of North Carolina–Chapel Hill. In addition to her on-the-job responsibilities, she recently completed a term as president of the human resources section of the American Library Association's Library Leadership and Management Association. She continues to mentor and coach current School of Information and Library Science students, write a career column, and cheer for her two boys (soccer or basketball, depending on the season). In her free time (as if!), she enjoys spending time with friends and family, wine tasting, supporting local agriculture, wine tasting, cooking, and wine tasting.

INDEX

A

More Great Books From Information Today, Inc.

21 Days of Success Through Networking
The Life and Times of Gnik Rowten

By Ron Sukenick and Ken Williams

21 Days to Success Through Networking presents a range of real-world situations, events, insights, and challenges through the eyes of a fictional character with whom almost anyone can relate. Gnik Rowten (that's "networking" spelled backward) has made a fresh start in a new city where he has few if any friends, prospects, or business contacts. Follow Gnik's life over a 3-week period as, each day, he discovers and learns tools, techniques, and strategies for effective business networking. By following Gnik's adventures and sharing his "Aha!" moments, you'll learn to extend, deepen, and effectively utilize your own personal and business networks in just 21 days.

176 pp/softbound/ISBN 978-1-937290-03-0 $15.95

The Accidental Law Librarian

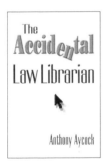

By Anthony Aycock

Where can I find the case *Simpson v. Satterfield*? What are the laws in Nevada on gun ownership? Can you help me apply for a business license? How do I copyright my name? Questions like these make a new law librarian's head spin. The truth is, all librarians are apt to get legal questions, and most struggle to respond. Collection development, too, is tricky if you seldom work with legal publishers. As the law touches more and more of our daily lives while lawyers price their services out of the average person's range, the public increasingly turns to libraries for answers. Where can librarians turn? Okay, that one's easy—to Anthony Aycock's *The Accidental Law Librarian*.

272 pp/softbound/ISBN 978-1-57387-477-9 $39.50

The Librarian's Guide to Negotiation
Winning Strategies for the Digital Age

By Beth Ashmore, Jill E. Grogg, and Jeff Weddle

Librarians negotiate every day with vendors, funding agencies, administrators, employees, co-workers, and patrons—yet the art of negotiation receives little attention in library education and training. This practical guide by three experienced librarian-negotiators will help you develop the mindset, skills, and confidence you need to negotiate effectively in any situation. The authors provide an in-depth look at negotiation in theory and practice, share tactics and strategies of top negotiators, offer techniques for overcoming emotional responses to conflict, recall successful outcomes and deals gone awry, and demonstrate the importance of negotiating expertise to libraries and library careers. The result is an eye-opening survey into the true nature of negotiation—both as a form of communication and as a tool you can use to create sustainable collections and improve library service in the digital age.

264 pp/softbound/ISBN 978-1-57387-428-1 $49.50

The Embedded Librarian
Innovative Strategies for Taking Knowledge Where It's Needed

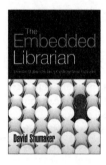

By David Shumaker

Here is the first comprehensive survey of the growing practice of "embedded librarianship"—a strategic model for placing information professionals into partnerships with the individuals and working groups that depend upon their knowledge and expertise. David Shumaker looks at implementations in all types of organizations, identifies the characteristics of successful embedded librarians, and explains how information professionals in public, academic, school, medical, law, and other specialized library settings are using embedded librarianship principles to enhance their work and careers.

232 pp/softbound/ISBN 978-1-57387-452-6 $49.50